# EARLY IRISH VERSE

# Early Irish Verse

Translated and edited by Ruth P. M. Lehmann

UNIVERSITY OF TEXAS PRESS
Austin

First Edition, 1982

Grateful acknowledgment is made for permission to reproduce previously published translations, as follows:

Nos. 2, 6, 7, 16–20, 60 (metrical translations only), reprinted by permission of The Modern Language Association of America from *An Introduction to Old Irish*, by R. P. M. Lehmann and W. P. Lehmann. Copyright © 1975 by The Modern Language Association of America.

Nos. 46–53, 63, 72, 74, 79, 93 (metrical translations only), reprinted by permission of the Board of the Medieval Institute, Western Michigan University, from *Vox Feminae*, ed. John Plummer (1981).

No. 50 (literal translation only) reprinted from *Etudes Celtiques*, vol. 15 (1978); nos. 5, 87 (literal translations only) reprinted from *Etudes Celtiques*, vol. 17 (1980); by permission of the Centre National de la Recherche Scientifique, Paris.

No. 44 (both translations) reprinted by permission of Max Niemeyer Verlag from *Zeitschrift für Celtische Philologie*, vol. 36 (1977).

LIBRARY OF CONGRESS CATALOGING IN PUBLICATION DATA

Main entry under title:
Early Irish verse.

Includes index.

1. Irish poetry—To 1100—Translations into English.   2. Irish poetry—Middle Irish, 1100–1550—Translations into English.   3. English poetry—Translations from Irish.   I. Lehmann, Ruth, 1912–
PB1424.E18   891.6'211'08   81-11669
ISBN 0-292-72032-7        AACR2

IN MEMORIAM
M.D. and W.H.

# Contents

Preface   xi

Note to the Reader   2

Introduction   3

   References   10

## NATURE POEMS

1. The Bee   12
   (*Daith bech buide a úaim i n-úaim*)

2. Blackbird of the Wilderness   12
   (*Ach, a luin, is buide duit*)

3. The Little Blackbird   12
   (*Int én bec*)

4. The Blackbird Calls from the Willow   13
   (*Int én gaires asin tsail*)

5. Calendar of the Birds   13
   (*Énlaith betha bríg cen táir*)†

6. Ocean   14
   (*Fégaid úaib*)

7. Storm on the Great Moor   15
   (*Úar ind adaig i Móin Móir*)

8. A Great Storm at Sea   15
   (*Anbthine mór ar muig Lir*)

9. Winter Has Come   17
   (*Táinic gaimred co ngainni*)†

10. Winter   17
    (*Scél lem dúib*)

11. Winter Cold   17
    (*Fuit, fuit!*)

12. Forever Cold   19
    (*Fuit co bráth!*)

13. The Worst and Best Weather   19
    (*Hed is annsam do rímaib*)†

14. Slieve Cua   20
    (*Slíab cúa cúanach corrach dub*)†

15. Summer Has Come   20
    (*Táinic sam slán sóer*)

16–19. The Four Seasons   21
    (from *The Guesting of Aithirne*)

16. Autumn   21
    (*Ráithe fó foiss fogamar*)

17. Winter   22
    (*Dubaib ráithib rogeimred*)

18. Spring   22
    (*Glass úar errach aigide*)

19. Summer   23
    (*Fó sín samrad síthaister*)

## DEVOTIONAL AND HERMIT POETRY

20. King of Stars   24
    (*A Rí rinn*)

21. The Wright   24
    (*A mo Choimdiu, cid do-génsa*)

22. Adoration of the Creator   24
    (*Adram in Coimdid*)

23. Tears of Repentance   25
    (*A Dé, tuc dam topur ndér*)

24. Writing in the Wood   25
    (*Dom-farcai fidbaide fál*)

25. Speaking God's Praise   25
    (*Mo labrad*)

26. Alone by Choice   26
    (*Glé limsa, a Choimdiu cen chol*)†

27. God's House   26
    (*M'air iuclán hi Túaim Inbir*)

Dagger indicates that the original Irish is found in the Appendix.

28. The Weary Scribe   27
     (Is scíth mo chrob ón scríbainn)

29. Colum Cille Leaving Ireland   27
     (Fil súil nglais)

30. The Little Bell   28
     (Clocán binn)

31. Prayers to Save and Shelter   28
     (Cid lúath cach gadur glan glé)†

32. Hymn to Saint Brigit   28
     (Brigit bé bithmaith)†

33. The Transitory World   29
     (Ná luig, ná luig)

34. To Find God   30
     (Techt do Róim)

35. Who Knows of His Death?   30
     (In ba maiten, in ba fuin)†

36. Mo Ling Offends None   31
     (Tan bím eter mo sruithe)†

37. Mael Isu O'Brolchan's Primer   31
     (A Chrínóc, cubaid do cheól)

38. Prayer for Protection   33
     (Día lim fri cach sním)

39. The Hermit's Wish   35
     (Dúthracar, a Maic Dé bí)

40. The Hermit   36
     (M'óenurán im aireclán)

41. Colum Cille in Exile   38
     (Mellach lem bith i n-ucht ailiun)†

42. Meditation Gone Astray   40
     (Is mebul dom imrádud)

43. Colum Cille and Guaire   41
     (Déna, a Gúaire, maith um ní)†

44. Guaire and Marban   42
     (A Marbáin, a díthrubaig)†

45. Daniel O'Liathaite Rebukes a
     Temptress   47
     (A ben, bennacht fort—ná ráid)


WOMEN'S SONGS

46. The Old Woman of Beare   49
     (Aithbe damsa bés mora)

47. Liadan Loses Cuirithir   54
     (Cen áinius)

48. Eve   55
     (Mé Éba, ben Adaim uill)

49. Little Jesus   55
     (Ísucán)

50. Lament for Dinertach   57
     (It é saigte gona súain)

51. The Sweetheart   58
     (Cride é)

52. A Girl Sings   58
     (Gel cech núa—sásad nglé!)

53. Loveloneliness   59
     (Och is fada atáim a-muigh)†


MISCELLANEOUS POEMS

54. Cat and Scholar   60
     (Messe ocus Pangur bán)

55. "What, All My Pretty Chickens?"   61
     (Cumthach labras in lonsa)

56. The Viking Threat   62
     (Is aicher in gáeth in-nocht)

57. A Splendid Sword   62
     (Luin oc elaib)†

58. The Necessity of Reading   63
     (Cid glic fri hailchi úara)†

59. You See Your Own Faults in
     Others   63
     (Cid becc—mét friget—do locht)†

60. Broad-minded Etan   63
     (Ní fetar)

61. Satire on a Rustic   64
     (Atá ben as-tír)


FROM THE SAGAS

62. Midir Summons Etain to
     Fairyland   65
     (A bé find, in rega lim)

63. Fann's Farewell to Cu Chulainn   66
     (Fégaid mac láechraidi Lir)†

64–68. Poems Attributed to Suibne the
     Madman   68

64. The Cry of the Sweetsounding Garb   69
     (Gáir na Gairbe glaídbinne)

65. The Snow Is Cold Tonight   71
     (In-nocht is fúar in snechta)†

66. My Night in Cell Derfile   72
     (M'agaid i cCill Derffile)†

67. The Woman Who Reaps the
     Watercress   73
     (A ben benus a birar)†

68. Suibne on a Snowy Night   76
    (Mór múich i túsa in-nocht)

69. The Cursed Banquet   78
    (In chuit sin chaithise in-nocht)†

70–71. **Ronan Kills His Son**   78
    70. Ronan with His Dead Son   79
        (Is úar fri clói ngaíthe)
    71. After Vengeance Ronan and the
        Hounds Lament His Son   80
        (Ro-gab Eochaid oenléni)

72–90. **From the Finn Cycle**   81

72–74. **Of Diarmait and Grainne**   81
    72. Grainne in Love with Diarmait   82
        (Fil duine)
    73. Grainne's Forest Fare   82
        (Is maith do chuit, a Gráinne)†
    74. Sleepsong of Grainne   82
        (Cotail becán becán bec)

75–79. **The Conversation of the Old
       Men**   84
    75. Caeilte Speaks of Finn   85
        (Dámad ór in duille donn)†
    76. Arran   85
        (Arann na n-aiged n-imda)†
    77. Well of the Strand of Two Women   86
        (A thopair Trága Dá Ban)†
    78. The Sons of Lugaid   87
        (Trí tuile)†
    79. Creide's Lament for Cael   88
        (Géisid cúan)

80–90. **From the Songbook of Finn**   90
    80. Beagles Bay on the Hill of Kings   90
        (Guth gadair i cCnoc na Ríg)†
    81. A Bell Rings on the Red Ridge   92
        (Faíd cluic do-chúala i nDruim Deirg)†
    82. The Death of Finn's Hound
        Conbecc   94
        (Trúag lem aided Chonbicce)†
    83. Caeilte Sang of Strength Departed   95
        (Bec in-nocht lúth mo dá lúa)†
    84. Caeilte Returns to the Mound of the
        Fian   96
        (Forud na Fíann fás in-nocht)
    85. Music of the World   96
        (Binn guth duine i dTír in Óir)†

86. A Dreary Night in Elphin   97
    (Is fada anocht i n-Oil Finn)†

87. A Grave Marked with Ogam   98
    (Ogum i llía, lía úas lecht)†

88. Oisin's Dream   100
    (Tuilsitir mo derca súain)†

89. Oisin Remembers Wilder Days   100
    (Ro loiscit na lámasa)

90. Oisin Laments His Youth   101
    (Do bádussa úair)

**FROM THE CHRONICLES**

91. Loch Silenn   102
    (Loch Sílend)†

92. Ainmire mac Setna   102
    (Femen in tan ro boí rí)†

93. His Queen Laments Aed Son of
    Ainmire   103
    (Batar inmuine in trí toíb)

94. On the Death of Aed mac Colgan,
    King of Airther   103
    (Ro boí tan)

95. The Drowning of Conaing   103
    (Tonna mora mórglana)

96. On the Death of Mael Fothartaig   104
    (Ní diliu)†

97. On the Death of Aed mac Colgan,
    King of Leinster   104
    (Int Áed issin úir)†

98. Cuchuimne   104
    (Cuchuimne)†

99. The Drowning of Niall Son of
    Aed   105
    (Mallacht ort, a Challainn chrúaid)†

100. Kenneth Son of Conaing Is Executed by
     Drowning   105
     (Monúar a doine maithi)†

101. Death of Princes   106
     (Rúaidri Manann minn n-áine)†

**APPENDIX: Irish Text of Poems
Not in Recent Collections**

    5. Calendar of the Birds   107
       (Énlaith betha bríg cen táir)

    9. Winter Has Come   107
       (Táinic gaimred co ngainni)

13. The Worst and Best Weather   107
    (*Hed is annsam do rímaib*)

14. Slieve Cua   108
    (*Slíab cúa cúanach corrach dub*)

26. Alone by Choice   108
    (*Glé limsa, a Choimdiu cen chol*)

31. Prayers to Save and Shelter   108
    (*Cid lúath cach gadur glan glé*)

32. Hymn to Saint Brigit   108
    (*Brigit bé bithmaith*)

35. Who Knows of His Death?   108
    (*In ba maiten, in ba fuin*)

36. Mo Ling Offends None   108
    (*Tan bím eter mo sruithe*)

41. Colum Cille in Exile   109
    (*Mellach lem bith i n-ucht ailiun*)

43. Colum Cille and Guaire   109
    (*Déna, a Gúaire, maith um ní*)

44. Guaire and Marban   110
    (*A Marbáin, a díthrubaig*)

53. Loveloneliness   110
    (*Och is fada atáim a-muigh*)

57. A Splendid Sword   110
    (*Luin oc elaib*)

58. The Necessity of Reading   110
    (*Cid glic fri hailchi úara*)

59. You See Your Own Faults in
    Others   111
    (*Cid becc—mét friget—do locht*)

63. Fann's Farewell to Cu Chulainn   111
    (*Fégaid mac láechraidi Lir*)

65. The Snow Is Cold Tonight   111
    (*In-nocht is fúar in snechta*)

66. My Night in Cell Derfile   112
    (*M'agaid i cCill Derffile*)

67. The Woman Who Reaps the
    Watercress   112
    (*A ben benus a birar*)

69. The Cursed Banquet   114
    (*In chuit sin chaithise in-nocht*)

73. Grainne's Forest Fare   114
    (*Is maith do chuit, a Gráinne*)

75. Caeilte Speaks of Finn   114
    (*Dámad ór in duille donn*)

76. Arran   114
    (*Arann na n-aiged n-imda*)

77. Well of the Strand of Two
    Women   114
    (*A thopair Trága Dá Ban*)

78. The Sons of Lugaid   115
    (*Trí tuile*)

80. Beagles Bay on the Hill of Kings   116
    (*Guth gadair i cCnoc na Ríg*)

81. A Bell Rings on the Red Ridge   116
    (*Faíd cluic do-chúala i nDruim Deirg*)

82. The Death of Finn's Hound
    Conbecc   117
    (*Trúag lem aided Chonbicce*)

83. Caeilte Sang of Strength
    Departed   118
    (*Bec in-nocht lúth mo dá lúa*)

85. Music of the World   118
    (*Binn guth duine i dTír in Óir*)

86. A Dreary Night in Elphin   118
    (*Is fada anocht i n-Oil Finn*)

87. A Grave Marked with Ogam   119
    (*Ogum i llía, lía úas lecht*)

88. Oisin's Dream   119
    (*Tuilsitir mo derca súain*)

91. Loch Silenn   120
    (*Loch Sílend*)

92. Ainmire mac Setna   120
    (*Femen in tan ro boí rí*)

96. On the Death of Mael Fothartaig   120
    (*Ní diliu*)

97. On the Death of Aed mac Colgan,
    King of Leinster   120
    (*Int Áed issin úir*)

98. Cuchuimne   120
    (*Cuchuimne*)

99. The Drowning of Niall Son of
    Aed   120
    (*Mallacht ort, a Challainn chrúaid*)

100. Kenneth Son of Conaing Is Executed by
     Drowning   120
     (*Monúar a doine maithi*)

101. Death of Princes   120
     (*Rúaidri Manann minn n-áine*)


Notes   121

   Abbreviations   121

Index of First Lines (Irish)   130

# Preface

This collection of early Irish verse attempts to give a representative assortment of poems in both a literal translation and one that imitates the metrical form of the Irish, thus providing some idea of the interplay of sound and imagery for those who do not read Irish. I have tried to check at least one manuscript of each poem, and I have also checked all the editions and translations that I could find. Of course the debt of my own translations and the Irish text to these is enormous. Gerard Murphy's collection has been a model for careful documentation, and his translations as well as Kenneth Jackson's and Kuno Meyer's have helped to make intelligible even the densest passages. David Greene and Frank O'Connor's anthology was useful for its spirited translations, even livelier than O'Connor's earlier and excellent collection of translations, and James Carney's versions for giving me courage to try an even more rigid adherence to Irish meters. Sean O'Faolain in *The Silver Branch* and Robin Flower in *The Irish Tradition* also show graceful turns of speech. But I have not intentionally borrowed, even going so far in the literal translations as deliberately choosing synonyms or secondary meanings unless the term used in another version was clearly the best possible.

However troublesome a poem may be, I have translated every word and every line, giving explanations in the notes if necessary. For my unconscious borrowings from previous work, I gratefully acknowledge my indebtedness. Nevertheless, I have not included in the notes translations unaccompanied by the Irish, except for those of Kenneth Jackson in *Studies in Early Celtic Nature Poetry*, where he includes notes on the text and explanations of his interpretation.

The imitative translations have been constantly revised as Murphy or Meyer or my own observation revealed other plays of sound that I had missed—linking of stanzas to one another by alliteration, assonance, or consonance, and the like. There can be no perfect rendering of the effects of one language in another, but the intricate sound effects of Irish meters are so unusual and so persistent that it seems well worth the effort to try to capture the music as well as the sense of the lines.

For most of these poems the Irish is available in the collections of
Gerard Murphy, *Early Irish Lyrics*; David Greene and Frank O'Connor,
*The Golden Treasury of Irish Poetry*; and James Carney, *Medieval Irish Lyrics*.
The Irish of less accessible poems is given in an Appendix, immediately
following the translations. Two late poems (nos. 53 and 86) are given in
the manuscript spelling of the fifteenth century, the rest in that of the
early thirteenth century, that used for the *Dictionary of the Irish Language* of
the Royal Irish Academy.

I should like to thank the University of Texas Research Institute at
Austin for making possible a semester's leave to extend the collection of
translations and to visit various libraries for checking additional manu-
scripts and editions. The library of the University of Texas has been most
helpful in giving me access to its materials and providing others on inter-
library loan. The staff of the University of Texas Press has also been most
cooperative. In London the British Museum Library made available the
most useful Harleian manuscript 5280; at Oxford the Bodleian Library
permitted me to work with the Rawlinson and Laud manuscripts (referred
to in the notes) and provided photostats. In Dublin I wish to thank espe-
cially Máirín Ní Dhomhnalláin, assistant librarian of the Royal Irish
Academy, who has been most helpful on many occasions for more than
two decades. William O'Sullivan of Trinity College Library for a like
period has been uniformly cooperative. In the Franciscan Monastery of
Dún Mhuire, Killiney, Father Bartholomew Egan spent an afternoon
helping me find what I needed among the manuscripts of the Finn Cycle.
In Stockholm the Kungliga Bibliothek provided me with a microfilm of
an Irish manuscript that was on loan to Lund, and in Bonn, through the
kindness of Karl Horst Schmidt, I was able to work in the Celtisches
Seminar, where Rudolf Thurneysen had gathered an excellent library for
Irish studies, some with his own notes. Finally I owe the greatest debt of
all to W. P. Lehmann for his encouragement and his example of intellec-
tual originality and achievement.

R. P. M. L.

# EARLY IRISH VERSE

## NOTE TO THE READER

A dagger following the poem title indicates that the Irish text is included in the Appendix.

# Introduction

In the early Irish period, the *fili* (plural *filid*), or poet, was the best-educated member of the society. He was no mere minstrel and entertainer, but had trained many years in the lore and the verse-forms of his people. He was closely associated with the keepers of the law and of the religion. He was a seer, a eulogizer, a counselor, and a teller of tales as well. In his stories kings regularly accord the *fili* deference for his wisdom, and he repays the lord with singing the praises of his illustrious line. We have tales too of importunate poets bringing the mighty into line by fasting before them or threatening satire—a weapon that was supposed to cause bodily affliction. Before achieving his position of power, the *fili* was carefully tutored in the traditions and tales he was to preserve and in the intricate meters to be used in the recitation. Only the foremost *fili*, the *ollam*, was entrusted with the full extent of this learning.

The early period was a time of oral tradition. Only with Christianity did a writing system come into use and poems begin to be recorded. We can sometimes guess at what the original age of a poem might be, but we cannot be certain. One possible indicator of age may be seen in numbers 83 and 88, which have been heavily glossed, suggesting that they were not easily intelligible to the generation recording them. At the same time, there was an especially esoteric vocabulary that poets might elect to use to dazzle the multitude, so that the necessity for glosses gives no absolute age. A number of the poems seem to have been recorded to explain words in one of the oldest texts. They occur in the commentary on the *Amra Colum Chille*. The verses, apparently, were well known and had preserved old words no longer recognized apart from these contexts. But later scribes were often clever archaizers, especially when the difficulties of the meter could be eased by the use of obsolete constructions. At the same time, metrical restrictions made it difficult to modernize the language of early verse, so that even in manuscripts of the Middle Irish period (1000–1500) we may find verse from earlier times.

Another source of poems consists of Irish manuscripts preserved on the Continent in monasteries founded or frequently visited by Irish monks. We have also treatises on Irish meter that provide examples of the forms. Some of these examples are single stanzas from poems we find in full elsewhere, but some were never more than a quatrain. There is evidence also that, when recording poems, scribes occasionally added stanzas, either of their own composition, or known from a source lost to us, so that simple and more elaborate forms may exist side by side.

It is difficult, probably impossible, to arrive at an exact dating for any poem. Whatever century one decides on, someone else will claim is too early and a third will claim is too late. Since to arrange the poems chronologically would separate poems that belong together by ascription or by subject, I have not attempted that, nor am I willing to take sides between the very early datings suggested by James Carney and the more conservative dates of Gerard Murphy and Kuno Meyer. The earliest poems here might be from the eighth century; the latest, from the fifteenth—essentially modern Irish. But following Murphy, Myles Dillon, and others, I have tried to follow the spellings of the *Dictionary* and *Contributions* of the Royal Irish Academy, since this will facilitate identifying words. In two poems (nos. 53 and 86) where we have only late manuscripts and the language of the poems seems little older than the time of the written version, I have left the later spelling unchanged.

Ascriptions are particularly suspect, for they require no revision of the poem, but could be the guess of a copyist at any time. Consequently, I have not recorded these or the short prose passages that introduce and follow some of the poems, just as I have included none of the prose tales in which some of these poems were embedded. Where the tales are involved, a very brief account is given, but inconsistencies in the stories indicate many retellings, losses of incidents, and similar tampering. At least one group of poems relate to the same persons, but the story behind them could be made intelligible only by a ready invention, and then, to be sure, might have little to do with the original framework. Some of the poems are clearly hermit poetry, in praise of the life of simplicity and isolation, or poems of worship and contrition. A few are satirical, a kind of verse the poets were adept in. A notable omission includes the eulogies and formal verses that endeared a poet to his chief. Nor have I included other similar verse of the later period, or the very difficult Bardic verse. Otherwise, I have tried to give characteristic themes of Irish verse. In variety, intensity, and development of form, it is an outstanding body of medieval poetry, capable of standing on its own feet without the support of a prose background.

The earliest Irish poetry did not rime, but was alliterative. In some of the tales these alliterative verses occur in the earliest form, usually with linking alliteration and with lines of nearly equal syllabic length. Later, syllabic length became fixed; a frequent length is seven syllables with a trisyllabic final word. This form of alliterative line was used as a mnemonic device for the laws—some of the oldest Irish preserved.

The origin both of the alliterative line and of rimed verse has usually been given as Latin verse, especially the hymns. But Calvert Watkins (*Celtica*, 1963) has presented strong reasons for believing that the basic line goes back to an Indo-European verse form, modified by the specifics of the language. Alliteration, then, developed, as it did in Germanic, after the strong stress became fixed on the initial syllable of nouns and adjectives, and on the stem of verbs. In Welsh, where stress later moved

to the penultimate syllable, *cynghanedd*, or the repetition of every conso-
nant in sequence, took the place of initial alliteration. The antiquity of
alliteration has been confirmed by its rules. These override the phonetic
characteristics of the consonants, which may be mutated or unmutated by
kinds of *sandhi* infection, characteristic of Celtic languages. Consonants
alliterate only with themselves, so that *nem* 'heaven' and *noeb* 'saint' will
alliterate with each other, but not with *a n-oíb* 'their beauty' or *a nduil*
'their creatures.' Lenition is similarly disregarded: *a ben* 'his wife' and *a
mér* 'his finger' will not alliterate, although the initial sounds are the same,
a bilabial fricative, and *ben becc* 'a small woman' will alliterate, although
the first word begins with a stop, the second with a fricative.

By contrast, rime—which developed later—rimes consonants by pho-
netic classes: stops, fricatives, and resonants. Even though the earliest
rimes did not always distinguish voiced from voiceless pairs, lenited con-
sonants were always distinguished from unlenited ones. Irish rimed verse
was the earliest in Europe. If, as some say, it developed from the Latin
hymns, it developed a long way, for in Latin usually only the final un-
stressed syllable is the same; when one does find a similar cadence as well,
it is not long sustained. Peter Abelard, composing Latin hymns in the
twelfth century, did not consider rime essential, although French verse
already was based on rime or assonance.

There are scattered examples of early rime in Old English. The "Rim-
ing Poem" of the *Exeter Book*, with its elaborate use of both rime and allit-
eration, the last part of Cynewulf's *Elene*, and scattered lines here and
there in other Old English poems show it might be used as an added
adornment, but in Ireland, perhaps as early as the sixth century, surely by
the ninth, rime and syllabic count were the principles of versification. En-
glish verse began to use rime with more and more regularity, but not until
the twelfth century, by which time French influence was strong, was rime
frequently the metrical principle on which verse was formed. The priority
of Irish verse in developing that principle makes it likely to have been the
source of European rimed verse, whether or not we see Latin verse as its
ultimate origin.

Alliterative verse persisted in Irish for prophecies, eulogies, and recita-
tions of genealogies until well into the Middle Irish period. Verse became
stricter in syllabic structure and even in permissible alliterations. At first
the rules were that any vowel (that is, absence of a consonant) alliterated
with any other vowel, the stops *p, t, c, b, d, g*, etc., with their mutations.
But *sp, st, sc* could be analyzed as *s + t*, etc., to alliterate with simple *s* or
other clusters. Later *sp, st, sc*, as in Germanic, could alliterate only with
themselves. The development from a looser to a more rigid structure oc-
curred in every feature—in alliteration, in riming of voiceless and voiced
consonants, in use of stress patterns with less free syllabic structure, until
finally in Bardic poetry, much as in Skaldic verse, the echoes of sounds
became so controlled that only unstressed syllables escaped.

If the development of rimed verse is obscure and the subject of much
argument, the relation of verse to music is even more of a problem. At
present the Highlands of Scotland and the Hebrides, where Gaelic is still

very much alive, preserve a number of old songs in a pentatonic scale, regularly sung in unison. They are chiefly work songs, similar to sea chanties. In Wales, as far back as we can be sure, harmony was abundantly used. In Ireland, solo parts with a choral refrain often combine both methods. In the early tale of the "Exile of the Sons of Usnech" there are several accounts of the brothers' singing that suggest descant, and of course there are similar implications in other tales as well.

Eugene O'Curry's *On the Manners and Customs of the Ancient Irish* asserts that the Irish made use of harmony, supporting this view partly by a careful study of ancient instruments in illuminated manuscripts and in church carvings. In the Spanish province of Galicia, where Celtic influence was strong, the cathedral of Santiago de Compostela depicts a choir equipped with instruments in the Romanesque arch above the head of the patron saint. Each figure has a different instrument: harps like the Irish harp, ones more nearly triangular, ones played on the knee like a zither, some with a considerable soundboard below the strings as in the latest reconstruction of the lyre from Sutton Hoo, others similar in shape but played with a bow, not plucked (or both), some played flat like a dulcimer.

Although several different terms have come down to us naming musical instruments, the application is mostly guesswork. We read in English tales of Tristram that he performed on "harp and crowd." "Harp" is a Germanic word; "crowd" is Welsh *crwth*, Irish *crott* (later *cruit*), usually translated "harp." Irish has also a *timpán*; the name suggests something like a drum or tabor, as it is often glossed. But in a number of passages it is clear that it was a stringed instrument. What we can be sure of is that the Irish had a number of different instruments besides the wind instruments that would acquaint them with harmony. We hear of the *ceis*, sometimes called a small harp or a part of a harp. Whatever the term may signify, a harp without a *ceis* is a frequent comparison for something worthless or incomplete. We also read of a "hole-headed" *ceis* or harp.

O'Curry describes a number of early stringed instruments that were so made that some strings, not bowed, could be plucked or would respond by sympathetic vibration to other strings played in the normal fashion. The haringfele of rural Norway is such an instrument. Otherwise, the bagpipe has been called on to support the knowledge of descant and also of the development of the pentatonic scale. But O'Curry notes also that a number of bowed instruments are represented with a flat bridge so that all the strings were bowed at once.

But is there a connection between these instruments and the poetry? Probably there is. Eleanor Knott (*Irish Classical Poetry*, p. 57) discusses the recitation of Bardic poetry and cites Edmund Spenser: "Theyr verses are usually songe at all feasts and meetinges, by certayne other persons, whose proper function that is." The poet who composed the verses—lying in darkness as he had been taught to do as a student of the art—found someone from the lesser ranks of the learned brotherhood to perform them at feasts and other ceremonies. Apparently the bard worked up the music and the poet stood by to be sure he made no errors. Furthermore, the Fenian Cycle survived in song and legend in both Ireland and Scotland, where the music with harp accompaniment was noted by collectors in the early nineteenth century. (See especially Murphy's Part Three of the *Duanaire Finn*, Irish Texts Society no. 43, where he discusses many aspects of this cycle.)

One final question may be raised, and one must answer it for oneself: What is the merit of early Irish verse? It is ornate, intricate, and artificial. The old alliterative lines are nearest to "the language of men," as Wordsworth calls it, and the prose is full of these passages—highly alliterative, often measured, sometimes marked with an *R* in the margin (for *retoiric*, *rosc* or *roscad*), as are many of the poems, especially when not clearly set apart by the copyist.

But the largest number of poems here are quite different from prose. Whitley Stokes, an excellent editor of Irish, working chiefly in India, finds the verse uncomfortably overblown, pretentious, lacking in real content. If "real content" means moralizing, engaging in intellectual discussions, or philosophizing, that is surely true. Beyond a doubt the echoing rimes and assonance, consonance, and alliteration are artificial. They are as artificial and give the same delight as Gerard Manley Hopkins' "dapple-dawn-drawn falcon" or "dapple, couple, stipple, finches', plotted, tackle, fickle, freckled, adazzle" in "Pied Beauty." But the regular iambic rhythms, standard rimes, and the like of the translations of the nineteenth century are no more in tune with modern tastes.

The two translations given for each of these poems try to convey the meaning, in the literal translation, and the sounds of Irish verse, in the imitative translation. No imitation, of course, can reproduce the rhythms exactly, but the imitative translations come closest to it in poems like no. 15, "Summer Has Come," where the Irish too uses many monosyllables. This poem and a few others in the collection are based on stress patterns rather than on syllabic structure. James Carney has ably re-edited them in *Ériu* (1971), a most important article for the history of Irish verse. In syllabic verse the rhythms vary from line to line, and no offense is committed in the translation as long as the result is a permissible equivalent. It is my hope that these translations will make it possible for those who are not Irish scholars to decide for themselves what the ultimate value of this verse is, without simply repeating what critics have told them it is like. The difficulty of the language and the intricate sound patterns of the verse often make it impossible to read for understanding and for form at the same time. But perhaps, with the aid of the imitative translations that focus attention on the patterns, the contribution to the development of rimed verse, the themes, and the forms can be independently evaluated.

In the imitative translations, the form, themes, images, and mood are the same, but specific words are chosen less for meaning than for the patterns of sound—alliteration, assonance, consonance, and rime—of the original Irish. In syllabic verse—and these poems are chiefly syllabic—it is not too difficult to keep the count of syllables and the characteristic rhythms of end-words. Fortunately, too, the original strong initial stress of Irish has reduced words by loss of endings almost as thoroughly as in English, so that it is possible to approximate the movement of Irish verse.

The accentual verse described by James Carney is not adequately repre-
sented. The underlying principle is not clear to me, so that I have thought
it best to omit altogether the poem "Mayday" (*Cétamain*). Other poems in
accentual meter—no. 15, "Summer Has Come," and no. 57, "A Splendid
Sword"—are treated as syllabic with the varying number of syllables in
lines noted.

The poems from *The Guesting of Aithirne*, nos. 16–19, are based on al-
literation with seven-syllable lines having three-syllable end-words. Al-
though this form is that of some of the earliest poems, these poems are not
the earliest in this collection. The form is more frequently used for formal
eulogies, prophecies, or the like, rather than for the essentially lyrical tone
of these four.

Besides imitating the form, the imitative translations follow Irish prac-
tice in riming classes of consonants, not identical ones. The Irish classes
are: voiceless stops (*p*, *t*, *c*); voiced stops (*b*, *d*, *g*); voiceless fricatives (writ-
ten *ph*, *th*, *ch*); voiced fricatives and lenited resonants; unlenited reso-
nants; and *s*. Earlier the voiced and voiceless stops and fricatives could
rime, but even by these freer rules, since stops rimed only with stops and
fricatives with fricatives, riming consonants observed the distinction be-
tween mutated and unmutated forms. Consonant clusters were very freely
treated. Among English fricatives there are more sibilants than in Irish,
and on occasion I have treated these as members of one class. Occasionally,
too, I probably have used *men/send* as rimes since that seems closer than
the Irish *mend/said*, but although the Irish treat clusters freely, the rime is
on the final consonant, not on another part of the cluster.

One other feature of Irish poems is the repetition in the last line of the
first line or the first word or at least the first stressed syllable of the poem.
Short poems usually do not follow this practice.

I have tried to avoid technical Irish terms for the meters or for the char-
acteristics of the meters, although early treatises on verse provide an abun-
dance of these terms. They may be found most fully illustrated and in-
dexed in Gerard Murphy's *Early Irish Metrics*. James Travis's *Early Celtic
Versecraft* gives an elaborate discussion of elusive features of Irish verse, and
there are good brief descriptions in the *Princeton Encyclopedia of Poetry and
Poetics* and "Celtic Verse" by Charles W. Dunn, in W. K. Wimsatt's *Ver-
sification: Major Language Types*. In this collection I have described the
meters in the conventional way—e.g., $3_27_37_27_3$, indicating the number of
syllables in a line (3-7-7-7) and the number of syllables after and includ-
ing the last stressed syllable of the line (2-3-2-3). In Irish these are one
word or a word plus enclitics, but I have had to resort to phrases in poly-
syllable-poor English.

The only Irish term I use is *deibide* (pronounced approximately
"davey"). In its broadest interpretation this merely means that a quatrain
rimes in couplets rather than alternate lines, as in most other Irish verse.
But a "*deibide*-rime" is characteristically one with the last word of the sec-
ond line of the couplet one or two syllables longer than the last word of
the first, so that a stressed syllable rimes only with an unstressed (as op-
posed to rhythmic rime, in which two stressed syllables rime). The lines

are usually of seven syllables, though the first line may be shortened. This form is the one most frequently used in Irish, but gives a rather limping effect in English. Nevertheless, I have also imitated this meter.

As used here, *rime* unqualified means end-rime. *Rime 1/3, 2/4* means that the lines rime alternately. *Consonance* refers to agreement of consonants by classes; *assonance* to the agreement of vowels. The qualifiers *internal* and *linking* refer to rime, consonance, assonance, or alliteration between two words in the interior of adjacent lines or to a word at the end of one line with a word in the interior of the following line.

The descriptions of the verse given refer not to the imitative translations, but to the original Irish, so that it is easy to see where the imitation departs from the original. The quatrains below illustrate several of the features discussed above. In careful verse no stressed word should interrupt an alliterating, riming, assonating, or consonating sequence, but only the strictest verse adheres to this rule. Sometimes an interruption is tolerated if that too rimes, or alliterates, etc., as when more than one internal rime or alliteration occurs between two lines.

a: alliteration; ir: internal rime; lr: linking rime; c: consonance

1. Daith bech buide a úaim i n-úaim            Bee, flying fast cup to cup,
     ní súaill a uide la gréin;                     sup in sun, hying from home;
   fó for foluth 'sa mag már;                    fair in flight toward the high heath,
   dag a dál, comól 'na chéir.                    nigh beneath come feast in comb.

   7₁ throughout; all endings of Irish lines consonate; rime 2/4

7. Úar ind adaig i Móin Móir,                  Numb the night on the Main Moor,
     feraid dertan ní deróil;                       not small deluge and downpour;
     dordán fris tib in gáeth glan               driving wind laughs, brays its best
     géissid ós caille clithar.                       above enfolding forest.

   *Deibide* with frequent alliteration; la: linking alliteration

23. A Dé, tuc dam topur ndér                 Wells of weeping God me yield,
      do díl mo chinad, ní chél;                    pay for guilt, venal, revealed;
    ní toirthech talam cen bráen,             with no true tear, my own soul
    nim náem cen anam cen dér.              unwhole—a sear, unsown field.

   7₁ throughout; all endings of Irish consonate; rime 1/2/4

56. Is aicher in gáeth in-nocht,
    fo-fúasna fairrge findfolt;
        ní águr réimm mora mind
        dond láechraid lainn ó Lothlind.

Bitter is the wind tonight;
it flings the froth-sea foam-white;
    no fear soothing seas today
    speed wild warriors of Norway.

*Deibide*

For the Irish of other poems, see the Appendix following the poems.

My hope is that these translations give some feeling for both the form and the content of medieval Irish verse. Most of these poems have been adequately edited and are accessible to scholars with a good library. Where I have departed from other interpretations, I have referred to articles explaining the differences in detail and if necessary have given a brief accounting in the notes. But the collection is aimed chiefly at those interested in the past glory of Ireland, at the time when it was one of the earliest European civilizations to make a cultural contribution to thought and literature. The Irish were unusually independent in their thinking, as can be seen here in the variety of metrical form and the appreciation of nature, of human love, and of religious devotion. Comparative literature and medieval studies would profit by recognizing this contribution.

## REFERENCES

Best, R. I. *Bibliography of Irish Philology and of Printed Irish Literature*. Dublin: The Stationery Office, 1913. *Bibliography of Irish Philology and Manuscript Literature (1913–1941)*. Dublin: Dublin Institute for Advanced Studies, 1942.

Carney, James. *Medieval Irish Lyrics*. Berkeley and Los Angeles: University of California Press, 1967.

———. "Three Old Irish Accentual Poems." *Ériu* 22 (1971): 23–80.

Dunn, Charles W. "Celtic." In *Versification: Major Language Types*, edited by W. K. Wimsatt, pp. 136–147. New York: New York University Press, 1972.

Flower, Robin. *The Irish Tradition*. Oxford: Oxford University Press, 1947.

Greene, David, and Frank O'Connor. *The Golden Treasury of Irish Poetry*. London: Macmillan, 1967.

Jackson, Kenneth. *A Celtic Miscellany*. London: Routledge and Kegan Paul, 1951; revised, Penguin, 1971.

———. *Studies in Early Celtic Nature Poetry*. Cambridge: Cambridge University Press, 1935.

Knott, Eleanor. *Irish Classical Poetry: Commonly Called Bardic Poetry*. Dublin: Colm O Lochlainn, 1960.

Meyer, Kuno. *Selections from Ancient Irish Poetry*. London: Constable, 1959.

Murphy, Gerard. *Duanaire Finn*, vols. 2 and 3. London: Irish Texts Society, 28 (1933), 43 (1953).

————. *Early Irish Lyrics*. Oxford: Clarendon Press, 1956.

————. *Early Irish Metrics*. Dublin: Royal Irish Academy, 1961.

O'Connor, Frank. *Kings, Lords, and Commons*. New York: Knopf, 1959.

O'Curry, Eugene. *On the Manners and Customs of the Ancient Irish*. Edited by W. K. Sullivan. 3 vols. London: Williams and Norgate; New York: Scribner, Welford and Co., 1873.

O'Faoláin, Seán. *The Silver Branch*. London: Jonathan Cape, 1938.

Travis, James. *Early Celtic Versecraft*. Ithaca, N.Y.: Cornell University Press, 1973.

Watkins, Calvert. "Indo-European Metrics and Archaic Irish Verse." *Celtica* 6 (1963): 194–249.

# Nature Poems

## [ 1 ]
## The Bee
*Daith bech buide a úaim i n-úaim*

The yellow bee is swift from hollow to
    hollow,
not insignificant is his journey with the
    sun;
good he is in his flight into the great
    plain,
his meeting is good, a feast in his comb.

Bee, flying fast cup to cup
    sup in sun, hying from home;
fair in flight toward the high heath,
    nigh beneath come feast in comb.

Meter: 7₁ throughout; rime 2/4; internal rime 1/2, 3/4; linking rime 1/2, 3/4;
abundant alliteration.

## [ 2 ]
## Blackbird of the Wilderness
*Ach, a luin, is buide duit*

Ah, blackbird, it is well for you,
in what bush is your nest?
O hermit, who rings no bell
your whistle is sweet, soft peaceful.

Ah merle, merry are you still;
    what berry bush hides nest, all?
Hermit, who will ring no bell,
    you sing well your soft sweet call.

Meter: 7₁ throughout with all end words consonating. Especially rich in internal
rimes: *buide/muine* 1/2; *clinn cloc/binn boc* 3/4.

## [ 3 ]
## The Little Blackbird
*Int én bec*

The little bird
that lets out a whistle
from the end of his beak,
clear-yellow:

Ousel sleek
pipes so sweet
from his beak
    broomyellow;

gives a cry
over Belfast Lake,
a blackbird from a branch
heaped yellow.

song flung free
o'er Loch Laíg
from tall tree
bloomyellow.

Meter: 3,3,3,3, repeated; rime 4/8, 5/6/7; consonance 1/2/3; linking alliteration
3/4, 6/7, 7/8.

## { 4 }
# The Blackbird Calls from the Willow
*Int én gaires asin t̄sail*

The bird who calls out of the willow,
beautiful is his bill, its call is clear:
sweet yellow bill of a lively black fellow,
a complicated melody he puts forth, the
    voice of the blackbird.

Bird that cries from willow tall,
beak is comely, clear its call;
    smart dark lad with sweet bright bill:
    lovely lilts the blackbirds trill.

Meter: a special form of *deibide* in which the lines rime perfectly. Abundant allit-
eration; internal rimes 3. All end words consonate.

## { 5 }
# Calendar of the Birds †
*Énlaith betha bríg cen táir*

1. Birds of the world, force without shame,
    it is to welcome the sun;
    on the nones of January, whatever hour
        it may be,
    a crowd of them calls from the dusky
        wood.

1. Birds of earth, pow'r without blame,
    give glad greeting to the sun;
    Janus' nones, whatever time,
        from woods chime their crowds and
        come.

2. On the eighth of the calends of April
        excellent,
    swallows come to their pure meeting;
    a strand of conflict, what hides them
    from the eighth of the calends of
        October?

2. Honored April eighth, they've flown:
    come the swallows flying home,
        strand of strife, what hides them
        then,
        from eighth October hidden?

3. On Ruadan's feast, a saying without
        meanness,
    it is then their bonds are unloosed;
    on the seventeenth of the calends of
        May
    the cuckoo calls from the tangled wood.

3. On Ruadan's feast—no forced word—
        they fly free from winter's bond;
    May seventeenth the cuckoo mild
        calls from wild woods over pond.

4. In Tallaght the birds pause
   in singing music on the nones of July
   for Mael Ruain, whom the Badb did
       not take to her,
   and the living pray on the day of woe.

4. In Tallaght birds silent cease
       to sing songs on July nones
   for Mael Ruain; the living pray
       Badb away on day of moans.

5. On the feast of Ciaran, son of the
       smith,
   the barnacle goose comes across the cold
       ocean;
   on the feast of Cyprian, a great counsel,
   the brown stag bellows from the red
       plain.

5. Feast of Ciaran, artist's son,
       wild geese wing o'er ocean swell;
   Cyprian's feast, counsel grand,
       from red land the brown stags bell.

6. Six thousand white years,
   the time of the world without
       misfortune;
   the ocean will break across every place
   at the end of night, at the cry of birds.

6. Six thousand of full fair years,
       age without grief of the worlds;
   seas will burst, all things be drowned
       at night's brim, at sound of birds.

7. Musical is the melody the birds make
   to the King of the heaven of clouds,
   praising the shining King:
   listen to the choir of the birds afar.

7. For heaven's King in the clouds
       birds raise sweet song with no words
   to praise the Prince in the sky;
       hark afar the cry of birds. Birds.

Meter: 7, throughout; st. 2, *deibide*, elsewhere rime 2/4; all line endings but 3.3 and 4.3 consonate (including 2); linking rime 3/4. (St 4 has been rearranged to conform to this pattern.)

## [ 6 ]

# Ocean
*Fégaid úaib*

Look from you
to the northeast,
the great sea
full of creatures;
house for seals
playful, splendid;
the tide becomes
full.

Look, there rides,
northeast glides,
torrent tides,
    teeming,
seals house walls,
wanton whales,
floodtide gales
    gleaning.

Meter: 3,3,3,2, repeated; rime 1/2/3, 6/7, 4/8; consonance 5/6/7.

## [ 7 ]
## Storm on the Great Moor
*Úar ind adaig i Móin Móir*

The night on the Great Moor is cold,
no mean storm pours down;
a droning, at it the clear wind laughs,
it roars above the sheltering wood.

Numb the night on the Main Moor,
not small deluge and downpour;
  driving wind laughs, brays its best
above enfolding forest.

Meter: *deibide* with frequent alliteration.

## [ 8 ]
## A Great Storm at Sea
*Anbthine mór ar muig Lir*

1. A great storm on Ler's plain,
fierce across its high borders;
the wind has risen, wild winter has
    wounded us
and has come over the great rough
    white-capped sea;
rude winter's spear has overtaken it.

1. On Ler's large plain storm is flung
past high borders, forsaken;
  wild winter wounds us; wind rose,
  the fierce swift seas it furrows,
by winter's darts o'ertaken.

2. The deeds of the plain, the plain of
    great Ler,
has brought trouble on our long army;
an exploit greater than all—no less—
what is more wonderful, indeed,
than the incomparable great news?

2. Play on Ler's plain, the sea's brim,
brings pain to our host striding;
  greater than feat or presage
  what more marvelous message
than this terrible tiding?

3. When the wind comes from the east,
the spirit of the wave is roused;
it wishes to go past us to the west
to the land where the sun sets,
to the wild wide green sea.

3. When from the east the winds come,
wave's wish is for free-motion;
  it desires beyond us west
  to lands where the sun seeks rest,
to wastes of wide green-ocean.

4. When the wind comes from the north
the stern dark wave wishes
to be against the world to the south;
against the expanse of heaven battle was
    given;
it would listen to a poetic incantation.

4. When the northwind drives along,
the wave's wish—frantic-strong—
  to besiege the southern world
  toward the expanse of skies hurled,
and hear sung enchanted song.

5. When the wind comes from the west
across the swift-streaming ocean,
it wishes to go past us to the east

5. When winds from the west shall wing
across salt seas, tide flowing,
  they long to go east of one

| | |
|---|---|
| to the suntree till it caught it [the wind] onto the broad far-distant sea. | to seize the tree of the sun on far-flung floods wide-going. |

6. When the wind comes from the south
   across the land of Saxons with war-
        shields
   and the wave strikes Skiddy Island,
   it goes to the corner of Calad Nit
   with fringed cape of gray-green.

6. When from the south the winds stream
   where Saxon shields threaten keen,
        on Skiddy Isle the waves beat
        to Calad Net's very peak,
   cloaked in cape of leaden green.

7. The ocean is full, the sea in flood,
   the ship-harbor is beautiful;
   the sandy wind has tossed eddies
   around Inber na Dá Ainmech;
   the rudder on the wide sea is swift.

7. Ocean full, flooded the sea;
   fair fold for ship seeking quay;
        the sandy wind sends eddies
        where the rivermouth ebb is,
   swift rudder on sweeping sea.

8. Sleep is not easy, a rude omen of defeat,
   with furious victory, with angry
        struggle:
   the color of swans has covered
   the teeming plain with its people;
   the hair of Manannán's wife is stirred.

8. No sound sleep—rough sign of strife—
   with fervent fury, hot fear rife;
        teeming plain and people hers,
        sweeping swanwhite mane covers:
   waving locks of MacLir's wife.

9. The wave rolled, strong on the stormy
        sea,
   across each rivermouth, wide toward
        the west;
   the wind has reached us, warlike winter
        wounded us;
   about Cantyre in the land of Scotland
   a flooded stream flows, a raging
        mountain.

9. Waves of wild water breaking
   rage past reaches deep gaping;
        winter war wounds us; winds come;
        about Cantyre of Alban,
   savage streams surge, steeps shaking.

10. Son of God the Father, with vast hosts,
    save me from the terror of wild
        tempests;
    righteous Lord of feasts
    protect me from the powerful blast,
    from Hell with its great tempest.

10. Son of God, of great hosts King,
    guard from ghastly grim storming;
        just Judge of feasts, prefer me,
        from beating blasts shelter me,
    from Hell's horrors' sting-storming.

Meter: A kind of *deibide* with the usual *deibide* rime in the first couplet, usually rhythmic rime (stt 1−7) in the second couplet, and a final line riming with the second line, i.e., 7₁ throughout, rime 1/2/5, 3/4.

## [ 9 ]
# Winter Has Come †
### *Táinic gaimred co ngainni*

Winter has come with scarcity,
water has filled the flat lands,
frost loosens the leaves,
merry waves begin to murmur sullenly.

Winter has come with hunger;
water fills flats once firmer;
    frost loosens leaf and berry;
merry waves start to murmur.

Meter: 7₂ throughout; rime 2/4, 1 consonates; linking rime 3/4.

## [ 10 ]
# Winter
### *Scél lem dúib*

1. I have news for you:
   the stag bellows,
   winter snows,
   summer is gone.

2. Wind high and cold;
   the sun is low;
   its course is short;
   the sea is running high.

3. The bracken is deep red,
   its form is hidden;
   the voice of the barnacle goose
   sounds frequently.

4. Cold has seized
   the wings of birds:
   season of ice:
   this is my news.

1. News is yours:
       stags call does;
   summer flees;
       winter snows;

2. Wind high, chill;
       low the sun;
   short its course;
       wild waves run;

3. Brown leaves blow,
       shapeless lie;
   frequent now
       brent geese cry.

4. Cold has caught
       wings of mews:
   ice age rude:
       this my news. News.

Meter: 3₁ throughout; rime 2/4; all line endings consonate in stt 1 and 3; st 2 all
but 3 consonate; st 4 all but 1 assonate; alliteration in eight lines.

## [ 11 ]
# Winter Cold
### *Fuit, fuit!*

1. Cold, cold!
   Cold tonight is the broad Plain of Lorg;

1. Cold, cold!
   Chill the night on Lorg's wide wold;

the snow—higher than a mountain;
the deer cannot reach their food.

2. Cold till Doom!
   The storm has spread over everything;
   a river—each sloping furrow,
   and every ford is a full pool.

3. Every lake that is full is a great sea,
   and every pool is a full lake;
   horses cannot reach across the ford of
      Ross,
   no more can two feet reach there.

4. The fish of Inis Fail are wandering,
   there is no strand against which the
      wave does not gush;
   among towns, there is no town;
   no hill visible; no heron speaks.

5. The wolves of Cuan Wood get
   no rest nor sleep in the wolf-den;
   the little wren finds no shelter
   for her nest on Blackbird brae.

6. The sharp wind and the cold ice
   broke forth to kill the birds;
   the blackbird cannot get a ridge it
      likes,
   shelter for its side in Cuan Wood.

7. Our pot on its hook is at rest,
   restless the hut on Lon Slope:
   the snow has smoothed the wood here,
   a while on Benn Bo [is] a hard climb.

8. Aged raven of Glen Rye
   suffers from the bitter wind:
   great is her suffering and pain;
   the ice that will enter her mouth.

9. Rising from quilt and down
   [take it to heart] is nonsense for you:
   much ice on every ford,
   that is the reason I say "Cold!" Cold.

higher than the hills, the snow;
no deer find food deep drifts hold.

2. Cold till Doom!
   Everything covered, storm strewn,
   rivers down each ditch on hill,
   ford and rill a flooded pool.

3. Wild waves each least lake grown full;
   a full lake each puny pond;
   horses cannot pass Ath Ross,
   nor feet cross, so deep beyond.

4. Ireland's fish wander the more,
   no shore there that no surge shakes;
   among towns, no town remains;
   no hill seen, no crane's cry wakes.

5. Wolves of Cuan Wood get no sleep
   and deep in their den no rest;
   no shelter wrens find today
   on Blackbird Brae for their nest.

6. Alas, the harm for a bird—
   wild winds stirred the ice chill;
   blackbirds find no ridge to bide;
   on Wolfwood's side of hill.

7. Our pot on its hook is still
   in the hill hut food seethes slow;
   snow smoothes this world's wood in
      time;
   hard to climb cliffs of Ben Bo.

8. Eagle of Glen Rye, wood rimmed,
   the bitter cold wind bites deep;
   great her misery and pain,
   ice, not rain, blown in her beak.

9. From flockbed and down to rise,
   a fool tires—heed what you're told—
   every ford freezes with ice,
   my advice in one word: "Cold!"
      Cold.

Meter: st 1, 2,7,7,7,; st 2, 3,7,7,7,; stt 3–9, 7, throughout. Stt 1 and 2, rime 1/2/4; stt 3–6, consonance 1/2/4, rime 2/4; linking rime 3/4 in all stanzas and 1/2 in stt 3–9.

## [ 12 ]

# Forever Cold
*Fúit co bráth!*

1. Cold until Doom!
   The storm is greatest of all,
   each fine furrow is a river,
   and a full pool is every ford.

2. The size of a great sea is every angry lake,
   each small keen company is a crowd,
   as large as the boss of a shield is each
        drop of water,
   the size of a white wether's skin is each
        flake.

3. The size of a pit is each dark puddle,
   a pillarstone is every level, a forest
        every bog;
   the flocks of birds do not find shelter,
   white snow reaches up to the buttocks.

4. Suddenly frost has closed the roads
   after a sharp fight around Colt's
        pillarstone;
   the storm has spread on every side,
   so that none say anything but "Cold!"

1. Cold till Doom!
   More than all, this storm would loom:
        the furrows as rivers gleam;
   at ford and stream, a full pool.

2. Each lashing lake—a sea strong,
   a throng each keen clustered clan;
        a shield's boss, each raindrop trim;
   each flake like skin of white ram.

3. Each murky mire—pit of rain,
   pillar, each plain; wood, each waste;
        no birdflocks find shelter fit;
   heaped white snow hip high is placed.

4. Sudden frost freezes the road
   since round Colt's stone struggle rolled;
        storm has gripped on every side;
   no one cried out aught but "Cold!"
        Cold.

Meter: st 1, 3,7,7,7,; stt 2–4, 7, throughout. Rime 2/4 throughout; st 1, rime 1/2/4 and 3 assonates with these; stt 2–3, all endings consonate; st 4, consonance 1/2/4; stt 2–4, linking rime 1/2, 3/4; st 1, linking rime 3/4.

## [ 13 ]

# The Worst and Best Weather †
*Hed is annsam do rímaib*

This is the hardest of bad weathers:
rain, snow with constant fog;
the dew and the clear bright sun:
this is the best of good weather.

Hardest this of foul weather—
snow, rain, and raw fog ever;
    best of weather, clear and fine—
the dew and the sheer sunshine.

Meter: *deibide* with rhythmic rime 1/2.

## [ 14 ]
## Slieve Cua†
*Slíab cúa cúanach corrach dub*

Cua mountain, wolf-haunted, rugged,
    black;
the wind howls around its glens,
they howl about its fastnesses;
the fierce pale dun stag bellows
in the autumn around it;
the heron screams above its fastnesses.

Slieve Cua: wolf-haunt wan and wild,
    wind wails along its canyons;
        they howl through hollows;
the hoary hart harsh bellowing,
    'round him yellowing autumn;
        herons scream o'er its hollows.

Meter: 7₁7₂7₂7₃7₂7₂; rime 3/6 (identical); much alliteration; linking rime 4/5.

## [ 15 ]
## Summer Has Come
*Táinic sam slán sóer*

1. Healthy free summer has come
   so the dark wood is bent;
   slim trim deer leap,
   the seals' way is smooth.

2. The cuckoo sings sweet music;
   there is smooth peaceful sleep,
   birds skim past quiet hills
   and swift gray stags.

3. The resting-place of deer grows hot,
   nimble hounds bay pleasantly,
   the white tract of shore smiles
   and the swift sea runs strong.

4. There is the noise of soft breezes in the
        top
   of the gloomy oakwood of Drum Daill;
   great groomed horses run,
   for them Cuan Wood is a shelter.

5. Green sprouts from every plant,
   the green oak thicket is covered with
        large trees:
   summer has come, winter has gone,
   twisted holly hurts the stag.

1. Summer's come, safe, sound,
       it bound the black brake;
   leaping deer, spry, slim;
       seals swim with smooth wake.

2. Cuckoos call—choir sweet—
       as we sleep, dream, drift,
   past calm coombs birds dart,
       the hart is hoar, swift.

3. Heat seized den of deer;
       "Good cheer" howled the hound;
   sea smiled on bleached beach
       where each wild wave wound.

4. Blind wind whined on mound,
       oaks 'round Drum Dell dim;
   great groomed stallions bolt
       in Cuan Holt shut in.

5. Green bursts on all herb tops,
       green oak copse of great trees;
   hinds hurt by holly run;
       summer's come, winter flees.

6. The blackbird sings a strong
    accompaniment,
  to him the wounding wood is a
    homestead;
  the fierce sad sea sleeps,
  the speckled salmon leaps.

6. Theirs the wounding wood,
    merles good music sing;
  strong sad seas asleep;
  flecked fish leap and spring.

7. The sun smiles across every land,
  it seems to me husks separate from
    seed.
  Hounds bay, stags gather,
  ravens flourish, summer is come!

7. To me husk slips from seed,
    on each mead smiles the sun:
  daws will thrive, a dog barks,
    harts will herd—summer's come!
  Summer.

Meter: stt 1–4 and 6, 5, throughout; stt 5 and 7, 6, throughout; rime 2/4 throughout. Stt 1, 3, 6, and 7, linking rime 1/2, 3/4; stt 2, 4, and 5, linking rime 3/4; consonance or assonance is substituted for linking rime in some stanzas. Abundant alliteration, consonance, and internal rime. James Carney discusses this poem with others that are accentual, not syllabic.

## [ 16–19 ]
# The Four Seasons
### (from *The Guesting of Aithirne*)

These poems seem to be intimately connected with the prose in which they are embedded. The form, unusual for descriptive lyrics, is the same in all four, and the themes are consistent with the story. The Irish seasons began halfway between our calculations: autumn began August 1, harvest time; winter began November 1, also reckoned as the new year; spring began February 1, the time of first milking after calving; and finally summer began May 1. Aithirne does not wish his guests to leave too soon, and in each poem but the last describes a season uncongenial for travelers. In short, he wishes his guests to stay until the year is up.

## [ 16 ]
# Autumn
### *Ráithe fó foiss fogamar*

Autumn is a good time for resting;
there is a load there for everyone,
throughout the very short days.
Speckled fawns from the bellies of
    thicket-does,
5 the red stalks of heather shelter them.
Stags run from their hillocks

Time of harvest, homesteading;
holdings here for everyone;
ever the days dwindling;
deer, flecked fawns from holtwood
    hinds
5 hide on plains of purple-heath;
proud stags, from hills hurrying,

at the bellowing of the herd.                    hearing bold herds bellowing.
Acorns, berries in peaceful woods,               Berries, fruit from forestland,
stalks of corn about the grainfield              fields of clustered cornstubble
10  above the earth of the brown world.      10      cover the broad bounds.
Blackthorn, prickly brambles                     Blackthorn, brambles—bristling;
beside the floor of the broken enclosure,        broken half a hermitage;
the hard ground full of a heavy crop of          heavy, crop-filled countryside,
    nuts,                                         cast by hazels, handsome nuts,
hazel nuts fall, an excellent crop
15  for great trees of ramparts.            15      high trees of old time.

Meter: mainly 7₃, occasionally 5₁. No rime. Usually linking alliteration, that is, the end of one line alliterates with the beginning of the next. I have kept this pattern rigidly in the imitative translation, and Greene and O'Connor have emended the text to bring it in line with what the original form might have been. I have adopted very few emendations, and those were all to keep the syllabic length of the lines, and the alliteration if that could be achieved without difficulty.

## [ 17 ]

# Winter

*Dubaib ráithib rogeimred*

Black season of deep winter:                     Darkest of times: true-winter.
flood-tide waves are lifted up                   Tides of ocean energy
along the side of the plain of the world.           on edge of world's wastes.
Mournful birds of every meadow plain             Woe to larks of level-land:
5  except ravens bloody crimson              5   look—ravens, red, ravaging,
at the noise of rough winter,                       as rough winter wails.
black, gloomy, dusky.                            Weary, dreary, darkening;
Hounds crushing bones are proud.                 dogs are bold at bone-crushing.
Bring iron kettles to the fire                   Bear to the fire food-kettles
10  after the dusky, black day.             10      for cold dusky days.

Meter: see no. 16.

## [ 18 ]

# Spring

*Glass úar errach aigide*

Green cold icy spring,                           Green, cool, quiet, quivering—
cold is produced in the wind,                    cold in the wind wakening;
ducks of pools of water have cried out,          wailing ducks on distant ponds,
fiercely complaining is the cranes' harsh        doleful cranes are chorusing.
    cry.

5 They hear the wolves on the wilderness;
on rising early in the morning,
the birds awake from the islands;
many wild beasts flee before them
from wood, from green grass.

Meter: see no. 16.

5 Calls are heard on highland moors.
Hurry, daybreak, dawning hour:
darting fowl from far-off isles
fleeing wild beasts, wanderers
from wood, waste, and green. Green.

## [ 19 ]

# Summer

*Fó sín samrad síthaister*

Peaceful summer is a good season;
the very tall choice wood is calm,
which not a puff of wind will set in
motion.
The hair of the protecting wood is
green,
5 the stream of rippling water winds,
in the good turf [is] warmth.

Meter: see no. 16.

Good soft season—summertime:
silent wood, wild, wonderful;
no wind blows but breathlessly.
Bright, fine feath'ry foliage

5 freshwell waters wandering,
warm on ground so good.

# Devotional and Hermit Poetry

## [ 20 ]
## King of Stars
### *A Rí rinn*

King of stars,
though my house be black or white
it will not be closed to anyone
lest Christ close His house to me.

Starry King,
black or white my house within,
   closed to none its doors shall be,
lest Christ close to me His inn.

Meter: 3₁7₁7₁7₁; rime 1/2/4; linking rime 3/4.

## [ 21 ]
## The Wright
### *A mo Choimdiu, cid do-génsa*

My Lord, what shall I do
with this great material?
When will these ten hundred boards
be a work of art of compact beauty?

My Lord, what should I be doing
   with this stuff abounding?
When shall these thousand beams
   fashion
   compact art astounding?

Meter: 8₂6₂8₂6₂; rime 2/4.

## [ 22 ]
## Adoration of the Creator
### *Adram in Coimdid*

We worship the Lord
with the famous works of art:
the great white heaven with angels,
the wave-white sea on earth.

Honor the Master
   and His art created:
wide sky bright with angels;
   tide, wave-white earth weighted.

Meter: 5₂6₂6₂6₂; rime 2/4; consonance and unstressed syllables rime 1/3; internal
rime *nen/ler*, *-már/- bán*, 3/4; frequent alliteration.

## { 23 }
# Tears of Repentance
*A Dé, tuc dam topur ndér*

God, give me a well of tears
as payment for my sins, that I shall not
    conceal;
there is no fertile earth without drops of
    rain,
I am not holy myself, my soul without
    tears.

Wells of weeping God me yield,
    pay for guilt, venal, revealed;
with no true tear, my own soul
    unwhole—a sear, unsown field.

Meter: $7_1$ throughout; rime 1/2/4; all endings consonate.

## { 24 }
# Writing in the Wood
*Dom-farcai fidbaide fál*

1. A hedge of a wood-thicket looks down
    on me;
a blackbird's song sings to me
    (a message not concealed)
above my little book, the lined one,
the twittering of birds sings to me.

1. Overwatched by woodland wall
    merles make melody full well;
above my book—lined, lettered—
    birds twittered a soothing spell.

2. The clear-voiced cuckoo calls to me, a
    lovely speech,
in a gray mantle from bushy dwellings
God's Judgment! The Lord befriends
    me!
I write fair under the great wood of the
    forest.

2. Cuckoos call clear—fairest phrase—
    cloaked in grays, from leafy leas.
Lord's love, what blessings show'ring!
    Good to write 'neath tow'ring trees.

Meter: $7_17_17_27_1$; rime 2/4; consonance 1/2/4; st 1, linking rime 3/4; st 2, linking rime 1/2, 3/4; alliteration in all lines but 1.4.

## { 25 }
# Speaking God's Praise
*Mo labrad*

1. My speech,
    may it be Thou Whom it praises
    without distraction:

1. My speaking:
    all praise on Thee high heaping;

may it be Thou Whom my heart loves,
King of heaven and earth.

my heart loves Thee, held faster,
heaven's Master, earth keeping.

2. My speech,
may it be Thou Whom it praises
    without distraction:
make smooth, purest Prince,
for me to serve Thee in all and adore
    Thee.

2. My speaking:
all praise on Thee high heaping;
    pure Prince, make paths unswerving,
Thee serving, Thy laud eking.

3. My speech,
may it be Thou Whom it praises
    without distraction:
Father of every affection,
hear my lays and my speech.

3. My speaking:
all praise on Thee high heaping;
    my Lord, all love refining,
hear my riming, my speaking. My
    speaking.

Meter: $3_27_27_27_2$; rime 1/2/4; linking rime 3/4; frequent alliteration. First two
lines the same in all stanzas; therefore all rimes are the same except linking rimes.

# [ 26 ]
# Alone by Choice †
*Glé limsa, a Choimdiu cen chol*

It seems good to me, O Lord without
    fault,
a poor life and being alone;
it would seem good to me as I wish
the absence of my friends and of my
    family.

Good it seems, Lord without sin,
alone and poor my living;
    I choose and like the life led
absent from friends and kindred.

Meter: *deibide*.

# [ 27 ]
# God's House
*M'airiuclán hi Túaim Inbir*

1. My little oratory in Tuaim Inbir:
a complete house could not be more
        firm—
with its stars in order,
with its sun, with its moon.

1. My small cell at Túaim Inbir,
    no full house is more steady;
stars, moon, sun are here assigned,
    by Him designed and ready.

2. Gobban who made it
so that its history may be told you;

2. Gobban raised that house on high
    that you might be told the truth;

my darling, God from Heaven,
it is He Who is the thatcher Who
    roofed it.

       little heart, God from the sky,
       He the Thatcher of its roof.

3. A house where showers do not pour,
   a place where points are not feared;
   as bright as in a garden,
   it is without a wattled wall around it.

3. House where falls no rain shower,
    place in which no points frighten,
   no wattling there that darkens,
   clear as gardens that brighten.

Meter: st 1, $7_27_27_17_2$; st 2, $7_1$ throughout; st 3, $7_2$ throughout; stt 1 and 3, rime 2/4, linking rime 3/4; st 2, rime 1/3, 2/4; some alliteration.

# [ 28 ]
# The Weary Scribe
### *Is scíth mo chrob ón scríbainn*

1. My hand is tired from writing;
   my great sharp point is not stout;
   the pen, a slim beak, spurts
   a beetle-dark draught of bright blue
     ink.

1. My hand from writing, weary;
    not smeary my quill right new;
   pen with its beaked point slender
    spurts dark splendor—ink bright
    blue.

2. A steady stream of wisdom flows
   from my good brown hand, neat and
     handsome,
   it pours on the page its draught
   of ink of grey-barked holly.

2. A stream of wisdom steady
    springs ready from hand fine-skilled;
   it pours its ink of holly
   (no folly) on page line-filled.

3. I send my little dripping pen
   across the collection of books of great
     beauty
   without pause, on the property of the
     skilled;
   and so my hand is weary from writing.

3. I send my small pen dripping,
    skipping o'er books of query,
   to grace great artists' dow'ry:
    my hand from writing, weary. My
    hand.

Meter: $7_2$ throughout; rime 2/4; linking rime 1/2, 3/4 except st 3 where end of 3 consonates with rimes 2/4; alliteration frequent.

# [ 29 ]
# Colum Cille Leaving Ireland
### *Fil súil nglais*

There is a blue eye
that will look back at Ireland;

A blue eye
looks back to Ireland—good-bye!

it will not hereafter see
the men of Ireland nor their women.

it will never see again
Ireland's women, nor her men.

Meter: 3,7,7,7,; *deibide* couplets with rhythmic rimes.

# [ 30 ]
# The Little Bell
*Clocán binn*

A sweet little bell
that is struck on a windy night:
I prefer going to a meeting with it
than into a tryst with a foolish woman.

Sweet wee bell
on a windy night ringing:
    that bell would I rather meet
than meet a woman sinning.

Meter: 3,7,7,7,; rime 2/4; repetition of dáil probably counts as linking rime.

# [ 31 ]
# Prayers to Save and Shelter †
*Cid lúath cach gadur glan glé*

1. However swift each sleek alert beagle
   hunting deer on this earth,
   swifter is the praying here
   taking souls from hell.

1. Though quick each keen, clever hound
   hunting wild deer on this ground,
       quicker is ev'ry prayer here
       saving souls from the hell-fear.

2. Sharp the many cries in the battle
   among the men of Ireland at Mag Rath,
   three times more in hell
   at slaughtering by the prayer.

2. Screeching screams from Ireland's men
   at Mag Rath, battle beaten;
       three times more cries from hell ring
       when prayers assault, ravaging.

3. Long singing of psalms in turn
   and the beatitudes of the clerics,
   to the demons whose hatred is great,
   though they are sung slowly or swiftly.

3. Ever psalms sung one by one,
   beatitudes most wholesome;
       demons are in hatred's grip,
       hearing prayers though slow, though
           quick. Quick.

Meter: *deibide*.

# [ 32 ]
# Hymn to Saint Brigit †
*Brigit bé bithmaith*

St. Brigit became confused in the Irish mind with the Virgin Mary and is
sometimes referred to as the mother of Jesus, as in stanza 3. The emphasis

on her virginity (stanza 4) helped in the confusion. See also no. 49 for a similar confusion.

1. Brigit, ever good woman,
   golden gleaming flame,
   lead us to the eternal kingdom,
   the bright shining sun.

1. Brigit blithe, bless'd may,
   bright, lively, lightest,
   lead us the bless'd way
   sunbeaming brightest.

2. May Brigit free us
   beyond crowds of demons;
   may she win for us
   battles against every disease.

2. May Brigit free us
   from fierce fiends swarming,
   see it swept from us,
   all fever forming.

3. May she destroy in us
   the taxes of the flesh—
   the branch with blossoms,
   the mother of Jesus.

3. Beat back within us
   flesh fees that feeze us,
   thou branch bright blooming,
   mother of Jesus.

4. The true virgin, beloved,
   of great honor;
   I shall be safe all the time
   with my holy one of Leinster.

4. True virgin, dearest,
   of high worth wholly,
   safe with thee nearest,
   Leinster maid holy.

5. One of the columns of the kingdom
   with Patrick the pre-eminent,
   the covering above beauties,
   the royal queen.

5. Prop of the kingdom
   with Patrick loyal,
   priced above princes,
   a princess royal.

6. After old age may we be
   with our bodies in sackcloth;
   from her grace may she shower us,
   save us, Brigit.

6. In coarse cloth dree it,
   body so be it;
   her grace will shower,
   our power—Brigit. Brigit.

Meter: 5₂ throughout; st 1, rime 1/3, 2/4; stt 2–5, rime 2/4; st 6, rime 1/2/4; much alliteration.

# [ 33 ]
# The Transitory World
### *Ná luig, ná luig*

1. Do not swear, do not swear
   by the sod you are on:
   a short time you will be on it,
   a long time you will be under it.

1. Swear not, swear not
   on sod you go:
   briefly on it,
   long while below.

2. Do not cling, do not cling
    to this world
    do not love, do not love
    a short space of time.

2. Cling not, cling not
        to this world near;
    love not, love not
        what's briefly here.

3. Do not ask for, do not ask for
    the slender life,
    do not seize, do not seize it
    nor fall down.

3. Seek not, seek not
        long life to spend;
    grasp not, grasp not
        a sudden end.

4. He was here yesterday,
    his appearance was bright,
    he is not here today
    except for blood under clay.

4. Here yesterday,
        his face, fair, sound;
    nothing today
        but blood 'neath ground.

5. It is in its course
    as the sea goes:
    flee from it far,
    do not rise, do not swear.

5. World on its course,
        like the sea there;
    fly from it far,
        rise not, nor swear. Swear.

Meter: 4₁ throughout; rime 2/4; alliteration chiefly in stt 3 and 4.

## [ 34 ]
## To Find God
### *Techt do Róim*

To go to Rome,
is great trouble, small profit;
the King that you seek there
you will not find unless you take Him
    with you.

Go to Rome?
    great pains, small gain will give you:
the King you seek there none find,
    unless you bring Him with you.

Meter: 3₁6₂6₁8₂; rime 2/4—probably accentual rather than syllabic with six stresses in each long line.

## [ 35 ]
## Who Knows of His Death? †
### *In ba maiten, in ba fuin*

Whether it be morning, whether it be
        sunset,
whether it be on earth or on sea,
except that I know that death will come—
great the loss—I know not when.

Be it sundown, be it dawn,
land or ocean be it on,
    my death will come, this I know:
the hour—woe—unknown till gone.

Meter: 7₁ throughout; rime 1/2/4; linking rime 3/4.

## [ 36 ]
# Mo Ling Offends None †
*Tan bím eter mo ʒruithe*

When I am among my seniors
I am witness that sport is forbidden;
when I am among crazy people
they think I am younger than they.

When I'm with those my senior,
not playful my demeanor;
 when I'm with wild ones that jest,
they think me the youngest.

Meter: *deibide* with rhythmic rimes 1/2.

## [ 37 ]
# Mael Isu O'Brolchan's Primer
*A Chrínóc, cubaid do cheól*

This poem was long thought to be addressed to a woman, one who had tested the sanctity of a novice by sleeping with him, as well as with others. This is the test referred to also in the note on no. 47, "Liadan Loses Cuirithir." But James Carney has proposed a more fitting subject, an address to an old textbook, found again after having instructed many others. Since the book contains moral precepts as well as hymns, it is probably a medieval primer rather than a hymnbook.

1. Crinoc, fitting is your music;
 though you are not young, you are
  chaste;
 we grew up north in Ulster
 when we slept together ever peacefully.

1. Your chorus, Crinoc, fit and clear,
 though not young, before us pure;
 we grew, keeping north with Niall,
 sleeping would seal peace secure.

2. My age when you slept with me,
 valiant woman of quick intelligence,
 a pure-hearted pupil, fair without fault,
 a docile little boy of seven sweet years.

2. Close together we two slept,
 valiant woman, wise in wit,
 pupil, pure-heart, without fault,
 exalt scruple, sev'n but quick.

3. We were in the land of stout Ireland
 without corruption of soul or body;
 my burning color full of love of you
 like a madman without temptation to
  evil.

3. Close in boggy Banba's land,
 body, soul, unsullied, sound;
 glad one's glances love will send
 but like mad one's lust penned
  round.

4. Your correct counsel is prompt
 for I chose it in every country;
 great love for your acute intelligence is
  better
 for conversing smoothly with the King.

4. Right counsel using, no less,
 that choosing, stress in each place;
 best seeking your wise words' hints
 for greeting the Prince of grace.

5. You slept with four men after that,
    after me, without any rash reaping;
    I know, the fame is vigorous,
    you are pure without sin with a man.

6. At last you have reached me again,
    after weary circuits, a wise struggle;
    darkness has come over your face,
    the last end of your life is without lust.

7. I think you dear without fault;
    you will have my welcome without
        limit;
    you will not let us drown in suffering;
    we find earnest devotion with you.

8. The enduring world is full of your
        speech;
    vast is your course over every path;
    if every day I followed your calling,
    I would come whole to powerful God.

9. You bear silent witness
    to everyone abundantly in this world;
    every day you sift for us all—
    it is no lie—[our] fervent prayer to
        God.

10. May the God of Doom grant us
    our time with you, our placid spirit;
    we delight greatly in the countenance
        of the shining King
    after our leaping from the withered
        body.

11. Take from me every small impurity;
    give me heaven afterwards;
    let the Man of bright heaven take me
    when I go after a long time from the
        earth.

5. Guiltless sleeping with four men
    without rash reaping therefrom,
    for far flies the fame you win,
    sound, with sin or blame from none.

6. Now, dear, you near me anew;
    dreary days through, wise your way;
    no lust has clouded your brow,
    now shrouded by your death's day.

7. Dear to me, fairest unflawed,
    rarest welcome, warm and kind!
    Save us from ocean of pain
    till devotion plain we find.

8. Fill with your words the wide world;
    tried and true each track you trod;
    if wending your gate on ground,
    then ending sound with great God.

9. Give your silent witness well
    to all in fitness this while;
    each day sifting for us all
    prayer lifting to God—no guile.

10. God of glory to us grants
    time for story, spirit's sports,
    delivered 'fore God's bright cheeks,
    as soul leaps from withered corpse.

11. Rend my every smirch and smear,
    send me to that sheer, sheen shore;
    take me, heaven's Helm and Star,
    wake me far from this clay core.
    Your chorus.

Meter: 7, throughout; rime 2/4; all endings consonate except 7.3; internal rime or assonance, usually of two syllables, 3/4 and often 1/2; linking rime 3/4 throughout, and in some stanzas 1/2; few lines without at least two alliterating words; the last word of a stanza alliterates with the first word of the next, except st 11.

# [ 38 ]
## Prayer for Protection
*Día lim fri cach sním*

1. God be with me against every grief,
   one [entity] is the noble Trinity,
   Father and Son
   and Holy Spirit.

2. The pure holy King of the sun,
   Who is more fair than any possession,
   is a splendid haven for me
   against an army of black demons.

3. The Father, the Son,
   the splendid Holy Spirit,
   three of them for my protection
   before the clouds of the plague.

4. Before sudden death, before swift
        death,
   before plundering of brigands—
   may high Jesus protect me,
   against the red sickness.

5. Against demons at any time
   it is the Son of God Who guards me,
   against sickness, against wounding,
   against thunder, against fire.

6. Against heavy smiting,
   against every other cruelty,
   may the Son of Mary
   bless my breast pleasantly.

7. Against judgments in Doom,
   Christ with me against every hardship,
   against weapons, against terror,
   against the poisons of the wind,

8. Against peril, against betrayal,
   against charms in secret,
   against disease in every way
   that is caused to the world,

9. Every blessing without grudge,
   every clear prayer,

1. God mine as fate twist,
      three divine, one host:
   God the Father, Son,
      and the Holy Ghost.

2. Holy King of sun,
      beyond all owned fair,
   my real refuge won
      from dark demons there.

3. The Father, the Son,
      Holy Spirit grand:
   save me, Three in One,
      from plague clouds at hand.

4. From being struck dead,
      from brigands of dread,
   me, my Christ, defend
      from the flux, blood red.

5. God's Son grants me care
      against demons dire,
   from blight, blows that tear,
      from fierce storms, from fire.

6. From sore smiting down,
      from all other pain,
   bless me, Christ the clean,
      my breast sweetly sain.

7. From judgments of Doom,
      from all ill, Christ mine,
   from blades, dread death's qualm,
      from wild winds malign,

8. From danger, from guile,
      and from secret spell,
   from what plagues assail
      this world for its knell,

9. Blessings without hurt,
      each prayer from pure heart,

every ladder that reaches heaven,
be a help to me.

each step to heav'n's court,
be my help, my start.

10. Every good saint who suffered
above the surface of the earth below,
every holy disciple
who believed in Christ,

10. All good saints who tholed
below on world's sward,
all disciples good
who worship our Lord,

11. Everyone kind, everyone quiet,
everyone sincere, everyone open,
every confessor, every soldier
who exists under the sun,

11. All kind and all calm,
all simple, all pure,
priests and men at war
who on earth endure,

12. Every venerable patron saint
who could help me to what is proper,
everyone simple, everyone noble,
every saint who has endured a cross,

12. Each worthy old saint
who leads me aright,
all humble, all high,
those who die for Christ,

13. Every noble stranger,
every rich one (famed for power)
every stark naked one, every saint
who leaves the country,

13. Ev'ry wand'rer wise,
all rich, famed for force,
all poor, all pure priests,
who leave lands in course,

14. Every tongue without fail
to which grace has been given,
every heart in the world
that never swears treachery,

14. Each unsullied tongue
where grave giv'n is strong,
each heart in earth's ring
that never swears wrong,

15. Every chaste righteous one
under the plane of pure heaven,
from the sunset eastward
to mount Sion eastward from here,

15. Each one, righteous, chaste,
'neath heaven the least,
from west to east traced
to graced Sion east,

16. May they escort me from here
from demons of fog,
companions of the King's Son
from the lands of the living.

16. Hence be they my guard
'gainst fog-demons feared,
friends of Christ who stand
in life's land, now neared.

17. May God be protecting me,
splendid Lord of angels;
the gift that came from Him,
may it reach Him whole.

17. May God be my shield,
Lord of angels bold,
whole may He then find
gifts He let me hold.

18. Let my King protect me;
may He save me on every occasion;
may I be at every danger
in the shadow of God's palm.

18. Protect me, my Lord;
be my staff and rod,
sheltered at each need
in the palm of God. God.

Meter: 5, throughout; rime 2/4 and usually consonance or rime between 1 and 2/4 and almost as frequently 3 as well. With a few exceptions, linking alliteration between the end of each stanza and the first stressed word of the next (not imitated here).

# [ 39 ]
## The Hermit's Wish
### *Dúthracar, a Maic Dé bí*

1. I wish, O Son of the living God,
   old eternal King,
   a hidden hut in the wilderness
   that it may be my dwelling,

2. A bright blue narrow stream
   to be beside it,
   a clear pool for washing sins away
   through the grace of the Holy Spirit.

3. A beautiful forest near by,
   around it on every side,
   for nourishment of many-voiced birds
   as shelter to hide them.

4. Facing south for warmth,
   a little stream across its land,
   choice ground with many benefits
   that would be good for every plant.

5. A few sensible men
   (we shall make known their number),
   humble and obedient
   to pray to the King:

6. Four threes, three fours
   suitable for every need;
   two sixes in the church
   both north and south;

7. Six couples besides,
   as well as me myself,
   praying perpetually
   to the King who makes the sun shine.

8. A lovely church decked with linen,
   a house for God of Heaven,

---

1. Living God, eternal King,
   my one wish alone:
   hidden hut in wilderness
   to be for me home.

2. A slim blue stream beside it,
   a pure pool in place,
   to wash worldly sins away
   by Holy Ghost's grace.

3. Bound by forest beautiful
   around every side;
   many bird-calls musical;
   they feed there and hide.

4. Facing south, warm temperate;
   the stream runs aslant;
   choice fertile earth, fitting land,
   planned for every plant.

5. Some young men of excellence—
   we shall count them there—
   as humble, obedient,
   they mediate with prayer.

6. Four triples, three times four,
   to fill every drouth;
   two sixes in chapel
   from the north and south;

7. Six couples in overplus
   around me the while:
   ever praying to the One
   who makes the sun smile.

8. A lovely church, linen-decked,
   heavenly God's hall;

bright lights afterwards
above pure white Scriptures.

above Scriptures pure and white
let bright lamplight fall.

9. One house to visit
for tending the body,
without ribaldry, without boasting,
without contemplating evil.

9. One house for guests handily
for bodily need,
no lust, no ill purposing,
nor surplussing greed.

10. This is the housekeeping I would get,
I would choose without hiding it:
real fragrant leeks, hens,
speckled salmon, bees—

10. This farming undertaking
good chance to seize—
fragrant garlic, hens freckled,
salmon speckled, bees.

11. Enough clothing and food for me
from the king of good renown,
my being sitting awhile,
praying God everywhere.

11. Enough my mantle and meat,
and seat may God give
to sit and pray in this place
a space while I live. Live.

Meter: less regular than usual; lines 1 and 3 may be 7₁, 7₂, or 7₃; lines 2 and 4 always 5₁; rime 2/4; stt 3 and 6, assonance 1, 3; st 1, linking rime 1/2; stt 4–5 and 7–11, linking rime 3/4.

# [ 40 ]
# The Hermit
### M'óenurán im aireclán

1. Alone in my little oratory
without a little human being in my
company:
dear would be a little pilgrimage
before going to meet death.

1. Alone in my hermitage,
with me there is none;
dear to me a pilgrimage
before my death come.

2. A remote lonely hut
for pardon of every error;
an upright, unblemished conscience
toward holy heaven.

2. Cosy hidden hideaway
to pardon each sin;
clear conscience, not lied away,
toward the holy King.

3. Sanctifying a body with good habits—
a manly trampling on it;
with weak, tearful eyes
for forgiveness of my desire.

3. Clean habits flesh sanctify:
spurn earth like a man;
weak weeping eyes pacify
and my passions ban.

4. Weak, withered passions,
renunciation of this world,
white, lively thoughts;
let it be seeking pardon of God.

4. Bursting passions withering
worldly life forego;
white lively thoughts, shimmering,
seek God's pardon so.

5. Supplications of sincerity
   toward the heaven of clouds;
   frank, holy, true confessions,
   a vehement shower of tears.

6. A cold, fearful bed,
   like the lying down of one doomed;
   a short, dangerous sleep;
   frequent, early prayer.

7. My food, my possessions,
   that would be a lovely captivity:
   my diet would not make me
   sinful, without doubt.

8. Dry bread measured out—
   good we cast our faces down—
   water of a bright pleasant hillside,
   be that the draught you drink.

9. A meager, bitter diet,
   earnest thought on [your] book,
   a hand against battle and company,
   a smooth serene conscience.

10. Dear would be the mark—
    a pure holy blemish:
    dry thin cheeks,
    leathery thin skin.

11. Stepping along paths of the gospel,
    psalmody every hour,
    bounds to talk, great tales,
    frequent genuflection.

12. Christ, Son of God, to visit me,
    my Creator, my King;
    my spirit to go to Him
    into the kingdom where He is.

13. Let it be the bounds that guard me
    among monastic enclosures,
    a beautiful little place, pure by art,
    and I alone there.

14. I alone in my little oratory,
    I alone indeed;

5. Sincerely then supplicate
   high heaven of cloud;
   may repentance culminate
   in tears wept aloud.

6. Lie on cold couch, terrible,
   as would one doomed there;
   short sleep, scarcely bearable,
   ever early prayer.

7. My portion and property:
   hardship that is dear,
   my meal without mockery,
   no sin need I fear.

8. Fetch brown bread proportionate
   then prone on earth sink;
   fresh flowing spring, fortunate,
   this the draught to drink.

9. Dismal, meager dieting,
   brood on books, mind keen;
   no visits, fights, rioting;
   conscience clear and clean.

10. Cautious signs show severally
    dear proof of heart pure:
    sunken skin, lean leathery,
    thin cheeks, chapped, past cure.

11. Come the course dominical;
    each hour sing a psalm;
    tidings—talk inimical
    to kneeling in calm.

12. Christ come, with me tarrying,
    my Maker, my King:
    my mind moves me, carrying
    to realms He is in.

13. At the house that harbors me,
    hallowed huts of stone,
    a monkish cell guards for me
    a pleasant plot alone. Alone.

14. Alone in my orat'ry—
    I all alone so;

I alone went across the world,
I alone will go from it.

alone I went through the world,
alone from it I go.

15. I alone, if I have committed anything
      of pride of the life of the world,
   hear my loud cry and wail,
   I alone, O God.

15. If alone I'm compassing
      pride, worldly life, fraud,
   hear my wailing cry, my tears;
   I alone, O God!

Meter: 7,5,7,5, except in stt 14 and 15, which Murphy gives only in his notes. Alliteration is abundant and alternate lines rime (except in stt 14 and 15). Furthermore, the last word of each stanza alliterates with the first of the next except for 14, 15, and 11, which Murphy also put in the notes. I have followed Murphy's choice of readings of the mss, since this best preserves the features of the verse. Assonance substitutes for full rime less often in the trisyllabic endings than in this imitative translation.

## [ 41 ]

# Colum Cille in Exile †
### *Mellach lem bith i n-ucht ailiun*

St. Columba (521–597) left Ireland in 563 and founded the monastery of Iona in Scotland. He was very famous as a missionary, part of his success perhaps due to his high birth on both his father's and his mother's side. Very likely he is not the author of any of the poems attributed to him.

1. It seems to me delightful on the breast
        of an island
   at the peak of a crag
   so that I may see the multiple
   face of the ocean,

1. Pleasant my place among islands,
        toward cliffs climbing
   to look often on seas sleeping,
        the shore shining;

2. That I may see its heavy waves
   above the broad sea
   as they sing music to their Father
   on their earthly course;

2. Looking on heavy waves welling,
        on wide waters;
   foam on firth sings to their Father
        as earth alters;

3. That I may see its smooth shore, clear
        points of land,
   no gloomy meetings;
   that I may hear the voice of wonderful
        birds,
   a joyous strain;

3. To see the strand stretched, light,
        level—
   merry meeting;
   hear birds' chorus, charming chanting,
        a glad greeting;

4. That I may hear the roar of breaking
        waves
   on the rocks;

4. To hear boom of billows breaking,
        restless motion;

that I may hear the cry beside the
    church,
the sound of the sea;

5. That I may see its excellent flocks of
    birds
above the great watery ocean;
that I may see its huge creatures,
greatest of marvels;

6. That I may see its ebb and its flood
in its running,
so that this should be my name, a
    secret that I speak,
"Back [turned] toward Ireland";

7. That repentance of heart might come to
    me,
looking at it;
that I may lament my many evils,
difficult to make them known;

8. That I may bless the Lord
Who rules over all,
heaven with its company of orders in
    purity,
land, shore and flood;

9. That I might study one of the books,
good for the soul;
at times kneeling for dear heaven;
at times at psalms;

10. At times contemplating the Prince of
    heaven,
holy the reward;
at times at work that is not oppressive,
it would be delightful;

11. At times gathering seaweed from the
    rocks;
at times fishing;
at times giving food to the poor;
at times in my cell.

12. The advice that is best in the presence
    of God—
may He inculcate it in me;

to hear the call by the churchyard—
    angry ocean;

5. To look on fine flocks flying,
    sea-floods sounding;
or look at the mass of monsters,
    sight astounding;

6. To see ebb and floodtide follow,
    this way steering,
that my secret name be given:
    "Face from Erin";

7. Lest my heavy heart be gnawing,
    if she beckon,
bewailing my wild ways many,
    hard to reckon;

8. Let me bless the mighty Master—
    bounty budding—
heaven bright with angel orders,
    land, strand, flooding;

9. A single book, mine to study,
    my soul calming;
now kneeling to holy heaven;
    now at psalming;

10. Now thinking of God and glory,
    purchase present,
now working—no forced affliction—
    that were pleasant;

11. Now reaping rocks for sea-tangle;
    now fish seeking;
now feeding poor ones, near famished,
    now cell keeping.

12. May God wake in me best counsel
    in His presence;

may the King Whose servant I am not
    abandon me;
may He not fail me.

keep me, King, I am thy servant
    in Thy plaisance. Pleasant.

Meter: 8₂4₂8₂4₂; frequent alliteration; rime 2/4; some internal rimes in stt 2, 4, and 8. Colum Cille's secret name (st 6) is literally "Back toward Ireland," with unfortunate ambiguity in English.

## { 42 }
# Meditation Gone Astray
*Is mebul dom imrádud*

1. A shame it is to my thoughts
   how much they stray from me:
   I fear the great danger of it
   on the day of eternal doom.

2. Through the psalms they journey
   on a path that is not proper:
   they run, they vex, they do violence
   before great God's eyes,

3. Through eager assemblies,
   through companies of foolish women,
   through forests, through towns,
   swifter than the wind.

4. Through pleasant paths
   at one time,
   through uncleared and difficult ones
   another time (no lie).

5. Without a boat in its devious way
   it crosses every ocean
   swiftly it leaps in one spring
   from earth to heaven.

6. They run (no very sensible course)
   near and far;
   after wanton wanderings
   they visit their own house.

7. Though one try to fetter them
   or shackle their feet,
   they are restless, forgetful
   at taking the burden of rest.

1. Shame to my imaginings,
   so greatly they flee;
   I fear their fierce ravagings
   when Doom reaches me.

2. Throughout the psalms fluttering
   on wrong ways, not right,
   running, vexing, muttering
   in our great God's sight.

3. Through thick throngs and tillages,
   women's bands that sinned,
   through forests, through villages
   swifter than the wind.

4. Through pleasant paths, neighboring,
   now they rush, they fly;
   then on wild ways laboring
   they stumble—no lie.

5. Without a boat, whirled winging,
   they cross the sea's girth;
   they bound in one spurned springing
   to heaven from earth.

6. No way of wise pondering,
   near and far they roam,
   after wanton wandering
   they come at last home.

7. Though one should try binding them,
   fettering their feet,
   restless, they not minding then
   to take time to sleep.

8. Edge of blade nor crack of whiplash
   subdues them effectively;
   slippery as the tail of an eel
   going from my palm.

8. Blade nor whip-blows whistling
   subdue them at last;
   like slick eel-tail glistening
   they slide from my grasp.

9. Lock nor strong curved prison
   nor any chain at all,
   fort nor ocean nor bare stronghold
   prevents their running.

9. Lock nor lone imprisoning,
   never chained to place,
   fort of foul provisioning
   nor sea checks their pace.

10. May it come, O dear, truly chaste
    Christ
    to Whom every eye is clear,
    the grace of the sevenfold spirit
    to keep them, to check them.

10. Let come, Lord, beloved One,
    Who finds all eyes clear,
    Holy Ghost's grace, honeyed One,
    curb my thoughts, these steer.

11. Control this heart of mine,
    O great God of creation,
    that you may be my beloved,
    that I may do Your will.

11. God govern this heart of mine,
    Christ of creatures, still,
    Your love be a mark of mine;
    I will do Your will.

12. May I reach, O Christ, your first
    companions
    that we may be together.
    You are not restless nor inconstant,
    not the same as I.

12. Join me to nobility
    who with You remain;
    steady Your stability,
    not like me in shame. Shame.

Meter: 7,5,7,5,; rime 1/3, 2/4. The meter is rollicking, with only four syllables in each line besides the riming word. In three-syllable rimes, occasionally assonance rather than full correspondence of consonants is accepted.

## [ 43 ]
## Colum Cille and Guaire †
*Déna, a Gúaire, maith um ní*

1. Guaire, do good concerning something:
   the treasure you see is like a fist about
   smoke;
   alone you came into your body,
   you will get something while you are
   alive.

1. Do some good, Guaire, no loss;
   this wealth's dross, hand clutching
   mist;
   into body 'lone you cross;
   yours no loss while you exist.

2. Son of Colman, scatter your property;
   fame is more enduring than treasure;
   he to whom God gives something,
   not good is a king, stingy in his life.

2. Colman's son, your savings cast;
   longer will last fame than wealth;
   him to whom God gives a thing:
   not good a king who hoards pelf.

3. Fine son of Colman of the troops,
    welcome is a generous one, woe to a
        grasping one;
    do not give heed to this life here,
    where every single man is only a while.

4. The kings of the earth, sad their death,
    unless they spend treasure and food,
    unless they themselves strive for fame;
    a hard, harsh man does not go to
        heaven.

5. Colum Cille the pure am I;
    little controlling in my own hand;
    from the day that I came into the body,
    I did only according to God's wish.

3. Good kin of Colman of bands,
    hail gen'rous hands, woe to mean;
    on life's ways here fix not faith,
    where each stays but briefly seen.

4. Worldly kings, alas their end,
    unless they spend food and wealth,
    unless for their own fame they fight,
    no hard, harsh men gain Heav'n's
        health.

5. I am Columkill the clean,
    my hand is seen empty, too;
    since the day my form was wrought,
    naught but God's command I do. Do
        good.

Meter: 7, throughout; st 1, rime 1/3, 2/4, linking rime 1/2, 3/4; stt 2 and 5, rime 2/4, linking rime 1/2, 3/4; stt 3 and 4; rime 2/4, linking rime 1/2, internal rime 3/4.

# [ 44 ]
# Guaire and Marban †
### *A Marbáin, a díthrubaig*

King Guaire and the hermit Marban were brothers. Guaire was widely known for his generosity, and there is a tale of his near impoverishment by demanding poets. Marban has to sacrifice to them his pet pig. But in return he exacts a punishing performance that the poets can barely achieve. When they ask for release, he extricates his brother honorably from them.

This poem is a conversation between the brothers in which Marban shows that his generosity to the wild creatures is the equal of any king's. Other translators, even Kuno Meyer after his complete edition of the poem, skip from the first stanza to the eighth. But it seems to me the humble legacy helps the contrast between the wealth of Guaire and the generous heart of Marban.

GUAIRE

1. O Marban, O hermit,
    why do you not sleep on a bed?
    More frequent for you was passing the
        night outside,
    the end of your tonsure on the ground
        among pines.

1. Marban of the hermitage,
    sleep in bed, not on forage.
    Mostly rests your tonsure's edge
        on ledge at forest floor-edge.

MARBAN

2. I do not sleep on a featherbed,
   though it be for my health;
   you are a multitude outside;
   thought escapes from me.

2. I rest not right on bedding,
   though it be my bettering;
   outside, how you crowd, you swarm;
   mind leaves me, unsettling.

3. Our fosterbrothers do not live;
   separation from them, you do not
       mention it:
   except for one half dozen only
   none of them lives, O Guaire.

3. No more live our fosterkin—
   loss unmentioned, though riven;
   except six of them alone,
   none, O Guaire, is living.

4. Ornait and perfect Lugna,
   Laidgen and Ailiran
   (it is a fresh lesson by means of poetry),
   Marban and Cluithnechan.

4. Ornait and Lugna the Long,
   Laidgen, too, and Ailiran
   (a lesson fresh through skilled song),
   Marban and Cluithnechan.

5. You have heard my testament
   at the time of coming here from the
       world:
   my cup of the hermit,
   my sow to Laidgen the feeble.

5. You have heard my testament,
   when this world's left for better:
   my cup from the hermitage,
   my sow to Laidgen leper.

6. My knife and my service, my dwelling
       in Tuaim Aidchi,
   my club, my sow, my cup,
   my house of skins, my music.

6. My knife and my management,
   in Tuaim Aidchi my dwelling;
   my sow, my cup, my cudgel,
   leather hut, music swelling.

GUAIRE

7. O Marban, O hermit,
   why do you will your cup?
   Because to the man of skill, his boon;
   but his betrayal to the son of Dui.

7. Marban of the hermitage,
   why your cup for conveyal?
   Men's hope for their skilled work done,
   to Dewey's son betrayal.

MARBAN

8. I have a bothy in the wood;
   none but my Lord knows it;
   from here an ash, from there a hazel,
   a great tree of a fort closes it.

8. In woodlands a hut of mine;
   only my Lord God knows it:
   ash here, hazel there now grown,
   great tree on rath to close it.

9. Two door-posts of heather for support,
   a lintel of honeysuckle;
   the wood around the chapel
   pours out its acorns on fat swine.

9. Two heather posts support it;
   woodbine for lintel narrow.
   Wood around the chapel close
   throws down nuts for fat farrow.

10. The size of my bothy—small, not
        small—
    a place of very familiar paths;

10. Size of hut—small, not small—
    place of paths familiar.

a woman in a cloak of blackbird color
sings a sweet song from its peak.

11. Stags of Rolach Ridge spring
out of its clear stream of the plain;
from it red Roigne is visible,
mighty Mucruime and Moenmag.

12. Little lonely lowly dwelling,
it has an estate of forest paths.
To see it, will you go with me?
I found it calm indeed.

13. Mane with twists
of the yew of gray trunk
(famous omen),
beautiful the place,
the great green oak,
besides that augury.

14. An appletree, apples
(great the good fortune)
big, fit for a hostel;
a fine crop by fistfuls
of the green branching hazel
with small nuts.

15. Choice wells,
falls of water
excellent for drinking—
they gush forth in abundance;
berries of yew,
bird-cherry, privet.

16. Lairs around it
of tame swine,
goats, pigs,
wild swine,
tall deer, does,
badger's brood.

17. In companies at peace
great hosts of the country
meet at my house;
into the fronting forest
come foxes:
beautiful is that.

---

On top in murky merle's cloak
one spoke in song like silver.

11. Stags of Rolach Ridge leaping
from its stream, clear flowing;
Macruime and Roigne red,
Moenmag outspread, showing.

12. Little hut, humble, hidden,
wooded ways for seizin.
Will you come to see it there?
I found it fair, pleasing.

13. Mane in tangles
of yew—gray-trunk—
omen fine:
region gracious,
green oak spacious
for the sign.

14. Orchard apples,
blessed bounty,
hostel fare;
harvest handfuls
green-branched hazel,
small nuts there.

15. Wells the choicest,
falls of water,
perfect brew,
gushing, welling,
berries swelling,
privet, yew.

16. Goats and farrows,
wild, tame, families,
come for food;
tall wild cattle,
red deer, dapple,
badger's brood.

17. Peaceful muster,
country cluster
gathers near;
toward the copses
come the foxes:
lovely here.

18. Feasts are finest,
    swine come,
    gathering quickly;
    pure water,
    crop for constant coshering:
    salmon, trout.

18. Feasts are finest,
    gathered quickly,
        swine come out;
    purest water,
    crop for guesting:
        salmon, trout.

19. Produce of rowan,
    black sloes
    of dusky blackthorn,
    food of acorns,
    bare fruits
    of bare slopes.

19. Crop from rowan,
    blackthorn berries,
        brown sloe sprays,
    food of acorns,
    naked kernels
        from bare braes.

20. A clutch of eggs,
    honey, acorns, heath-pease
    (it is God Who sent it)
    sweet apples,
    red bogberries,
    bilberries.

20. Eggs and honey,
    acorns, heath-pease
        (God lets shed);
    sweetest apples,
    bright bogberries,
        whortles red.

21. Beer with herbs,
    a place for strawberries,
    good tasting plants,
    haws of hawthorn,
    yew-berries,
    sloes, nuts.

21. Berries strewing,
    spicy brewing,
        tasty cups,
    haws of fruittrees,
    seeds from yewtrees,
        sloes and nuts.

22. A cup of mead
    of fine hazel
    quickly poured out;
    brown oak saplings,
    manes of brambles
    of good berries.

22. Hazel flavored
    fine mead flagon
        quickly poured;
    brown oak saplings,
    manes of brambles:
        fair fruit hoard.

23. When summer comes—
    lovely-colored mantle—
    delicious flavor,
    cucumber, oregano,
    hair of a stream,
    green crystal.

23. Then comes summer,
    soft bright mantle,
        savor keen:
    marj'ram, gherkin,
    lurking cresses,
        stream glass green.

24. Sounds of doves
    of bright breasts,
    profitable hunting;
    singing of a thrush,
    familiar weeping
    above my house.

24. Doves that murmur,
    breasts are brilliant—
        happy hunt—
    thrushes haunting
    cry of longing
        o'er my hut.

25. Bees, beetles,
      humming of the world,
      gentle crooning:
      barnacle geese, brants,
      shortly before the beginning of winter,
      music of a dark torrent.

26. A lively songster,
      fussy brown wren,
      on the hazel bough;
      in a piebald hood
      the woodpecker on an oak
      in a great crowd.

27. Fair white ones come,
      cranes, gulls;
      the coast sings to them;
      no mournful music
      of the grey-brown hen
      in the russet heather.

28. Heifers are noisy
      in summer of loud thunder,
      lightning storm;
      not bitter nor toilsome
      above the soft,
      pleasant, level plain.

29. Voice of the wind
      toward the branching wood,
      a very gray cloud;
      falls in the river,
      trumpeting swans:
      beautiful music.

30. A beautiful pine
      makes music for me
      not having been bought;
      to Christ each fault
      is no worse for me
      than for you.

31. Though you are pleased
      with what you enjoy
      more than any treasure,
      I am grateful
      for what is given me
      by my fair Christ.

25. Bee swarms, beetles,
      earthly humming,
      gentle croon;
      brent geese, ganders,
      winter clamors,
      sings dark flume,

26. Songsters hustle,
      brown wrens bustle,
      hop on high;
      hood in checker
      oakwood pecker—
      great flocks fly.

27. Fair white flyers,
      cranes, gulls—cryers—
      rough coast roars;
      no sad mourning,
      heath-hen calling
      on red moors.

28. Cows low, summer
      of loud thunder,
      light aloft;
      no harm present
      on plains pleasant,
      level, soft.

29. Wind's voice ranting
      to woods branching,
      gray clouds throng;
      water falling,
      wild swans wailing:
      lovely song.

30. Fair the pinetree
      to me singing—
      no pay due—
      to Christ faults be
      no worse for me
      than for you.

31. Though you favor
      more than treasure
      what you find,
      to me liefer
      what may offer
      Christ so kind.

32. Without a time of combat,
    without the din of battle
    that assails me,
    I am grateful to the Prince
    Who gives each good
    to me in my hut.

32. Never quarrel,
    never clamor
        that may strike,
    I thank my Lord
    for each award,
        mine tonight.

GUAIRE

33. I will give my splendid kingdom
    with my share of Colman's patrimony
    in undisputed possession to the hour of
        my death
    for being in your company, O Marban.

33. I will give my royal realm,
        my patrimony carven,
    entailed to my dying day
        to stay beside you, Marban.

Meter: Stt 1, 3, 7, 7,7,7,7₂; rime 2/4; stt 1 and 3, consonance all lines; stt 1 and 7, linking rime 3/4; st 1, final syllables rime though only line 3 is stressed.

St 2, 7₂7,7,7₃; rime 2/4; linking rime 3/4; consonance all lines.

St 4, 7,7,7,7₃; rime 1/3, 2/4 but related to *deibide* since the stressed rimes 1/3 rime with the finals of 2/4.

St 5, 7,7₂7,7₂; rime 2/4.

St 6, 7,7₂7,7₂; rime 2/4.

Stt 8, 10, 33, 7,7,7,7₂; rime 2/4; st 8, consonance 1/3; stt 10 and 33, linking rime 3/4; st 10, alliteration every line.

St 9, 7₂7₂7,7₂; rime 2/4; linking rime 3/4.

Stt 11–12, 7₂6,7,6₂; rime 2/4; linking rime 3/4.

Stt 13–29, 31, 4₂4₂3,4₂4₂3,; rime 3/6 in all these; rime 1/2 in stt 17, 21, 26–28; rime 4/5 in stt 15–17, 21–22, 24–28; st 13, assonance of unstressed syllables 1/2, full assonance 4/5; stt 14, 19, 20, 23, much alliteration; st 23, linking rime 4/5; st 29, consonance and near rime 4/5; st 31, near rime 4/5. In st 18, alternate reading of line 1 gives fair rime 1/2. First three lines then:

Chieftains stunning,
swine come running,
    crowd about.

Stt 30, 32, 4₂4₂3,4,4,3,; rime 3/6, 4/5.

# [ 45 ]
# Daniel O'Liathaite Rebukes a Temptress
## *A ben, bennacht fort—ná ráid*

Daniel O'Liathaite was abbot of Lismore in the middle of the ninth century; he died in 863. Gerard Murphy believes that the poem may indeed be that early, though we find the earliest version in the *Book of Leinster*, twelfth century. Murphy corrects meters and rimes of some lines by suggesting Old Irish forms for some of the Middle Irish ones.

1. Woman, bless you—do not speak!
   Consider the tryst with eternal doom

1. Bless you, woman, speak no more;
       think that sore long doom comes
           near;

There is decay for all creatures:
I fear to go into cold clay.

every creature must decay;
cold clay forever I fear.

2. You consider folly that is without
      value:
   it is well known it is not wisdom that
      you practice.
   What you say will be empty talk:
   our death will be nearer before it
      occurs.

2. You think of profitless joy,
      clearly no wise ploy for you;
   empty speech is what you say;
      each day death nears for us two.

3. Let us recall the destiny
   that approaches us (a limited course):
   here should we give pain to the King,
   we shall repent it in the land beyond.

3. The end before us comes soon;
      short way to doom, understand:
   if here we cause the King pain,
      the same ours in yonder land.

4. I do not sell heaven for sin;
   if I do it will be repaid me.
   What you will not find afterwards,
   O woman, do not give it for a crime.

4. I sell not heaven for sin;
      too high the price, little gain;
   utter loss to trade for crime:
      a soul paid for time of blame.

5. Cast it from you so that you will have
   your share in heaven, do not sell it;
   under the protection of God, go to your
      home;
   take a blessing from me, O woman.

5. Cast from you what gives you hurt;
      of heaven, sell not your part;
   go home, woman, in God's care,
      a blessing bear from my heart.

6. I and you, you and I,
   I fear, let you fear the day of the good
      Lord;
   pray you, I shall pray the holy Master;
   O woman, say nothing more.

6. I, you—you, I—stand in awe,
      fearing good God Whom we pray;
   Lord of love, we two implore—
      woman, no more you may say.

7. Be not hunting what is not good,
   for the Lord will cast you to death;
   fear, I fear Christ without sin
   Whose curse I have not dared [to
      incur], O woman.

7. Hunt not evil for the Prince
      will cast you hence: go, confess!
   fear—I fear—the sinless Son,
      the One Who may curse or bless.
      Bless.

Meter: 7₁ throughout; rime 2/4; linking rime 3/4 and 1/2 or consonance 1/2/4
or both; internal rime stt 2, 4, 7.

# Women's Songs

## [ 46 ]
## The Old Woman of Beare
*Aithbe damsa bés mora*

The old woman, or nun, of Beare is thought to be an ancient earth-figure. Some, too, have thought she personified sovereignty, often represented as a woman. She may have been both or, like François Villon's "Belle Heaulmière," simply an old woman recalling her youth when she had many lovers. But this poem belongs to the Christian period. The speaker remembers with pleasure her attractive and amorous youth, but looks forward to salvation as now her frivolities have gone with her beauty.

1. Ebb to me in the way of the sea;
   old age makes me brown;
   though I may grieve at it,
   it is lucky its feast comes [with the
       returning tide].

1. Ebbing I, unlike ocean;
   old age has made me sallow;
   although for that I grieve
   glad sea-feast fills the shallow.

2. I am Bui, the Old Woman [or the
       Nun] of Beare;
   I used to wear ever-new linen;
   today I have become so thin,
   I could not wear out even a worn shirt.

2. Bui am I, of Beara nun,
   once clad in stuff new woven;
   today I am grown so thin
   I'd not wear out old linen.

3. They are riches
   that are loved by you, they are not people;
   as for us, while we lived
   there were people that we loved.

3. Not people
   you love, but wealth—the cheaper;
   but we, living meagerly,
   loved people more eagerly.

4. Dear were the people
   whose plains we rode across;
   it was well we enjoyed ourselves among
       them;
   it was little they promised afterwards.

4. Beloved were the people
   whose plains we rode with laughter;
   good the time we spent with them,
   little they promised after.

5. Today they make fine claims,
   and it is not much that they lent;

5. Today they claim merrily,
   but not much have they yielded;

though they give little,
   great was the amount they promised.

6. Swift chariots
   and horses that won the prize,
   a while there was a flood of them:
   bless the King who gave them!

7. My body bitterly makes its way
   toward the mansions where it is known:
   when it seems timely to the Son of God
   let Him come to receive his loan.

8. My hands are bony and thin
   when they are seen;—
   dear was the art they performed:
   they used to be about great kings.

9. When my arms are seen
   bony and thin they are;
   indeed, they are unworthy to raise
   up over handsome boys.

10. The girls rejoice
    when Mayday comes to them;
    for me grief is more suitable:
    besides being sad, I am an old woman.

11. I pour forth no honeyed speeches;
    no wethers are killed for my wedding;
    my locks are few and gray;
    it is no grief to have a mean veil over
        them.

12. It does not seem ill to me
    to be with a white veil on my head;
    there was many a covering of every
        color
    on my head as I drank good ale.

13. I envy nothing old
    except only Feimen:
    as for me, I have spent that completely;
    Feimen's top is still yellow.

14. The stone of the kings on Feimen,
    Ronan's seat in Bregun,

though small our gain verily,
   a great lot they conceded.

6. Racing steeds,
   prize chariots for their speeds,
   once a flood of them they'd bring;
   bless the King who gave me these.

7. My body fiercely making
   toward due acknowledged rating;
   when it seems time to God's Son,
   let Him come, loans retaking.

8. Look at my arms, all scrawny,
   skinny and thin and bony!
   Dear was the art that graced 'em,
   embracing great kings wholly.

9. Skinny and thin and bony,
   look at my arms all scrawny!
   unfit to raise, though humbly,
   round comely boys and brawny.

10. Joyful are all the maidens
    when comes the time of Mayday;
    more fitting for me my moan,
    old crone long past my heyday.

11. No honeyed words I'm saying;
    no wethers for my wedding;
    scant my locks, pale and graying;
    a mean veil I'm not dreading.

12. No tears shed
    at this white veil on my head;
    scarves of all colors glinting
    on my head at ale-drinking.

13. Naught old I envy but this:
    Old Feimen's fertile surface;
    I spent that all—naught to show—
    Feimen's crop is still yellow.

14. On Feimen stands the Kings' Stone;
    Ronan's dwelling on Bregun;

it is long since storms reached
their cheeks, but they are not old,
    withered.

long since storms have struck each one,
but their cheeks aren't old,
    shrunken.

15. The wave of the great sea is noisy;
the winter has begun to lift it:
neither nobleman nor slave's son today
do I expect to visit.

15. The waves of the great sea stir;
storms rouse the roar of winter;
no nobleman nor slave's son
will come here today—no one.

16. I know what they are doing:
they row back and forth;
the reeds of the Ford of Allen,
it is cold the dwelling where they are.

16. I know what they are doing:
back and forth they are rowing;
    (Ath Allen—reed and lily)
to chilly sleep they're going.

17. It is many a day
since I sailed on the sea of youth!
Many years of my beauty have gone
for my lust has been used up.

17. Many days
since I sailed on youth's seaways;
    many years with beauty gone;
    spent are my days as wanton.

18. It is many a day
for me today, whatever comes,
I take my shawl though in the sun:*
age is on me; I myself know it.

18. Many days
whatever come, though suns blaze;
    shawl I wear where'er I go:
    old age is mine—that I know.

19. Summer of youth in which we were
I have spent, with its autumn;
winter of age drowns everyone,
its early months approach me.

19. I have spent youth's summertime
and autumn, that other time;
    in winter of age men drown;
    its first frost comes—my sundown.

20. I spent my youth in the beginning;
I am glad that I so chose:
though my leap over the wall was small,
the cloak would not still be new.

20. Soon my youth I wasted, cropped;
    I think good the course I kept:
old would be my cloak though small
    the wall over which I leapt.

21. Beautiful is the green cloak
that my King has spread over Drumain;
noble is the Fuller Who treads it:
He has given it wool after rough cloth.

21. Fair is the fine cloak greening
    hills where my God spreads it;
nobly that cloak He's cleaning:
    wool hides bare ground, He treads it.

22. Indeed I am very cold;
each eye deteriorates.
After feasts with bright candles,
being in the dark of a chapel.

22. I'm wretched, alas for me,
    each fair eye is darkening;
since feasts with lights a-dapple,
    chapel's gloom disheartening.

23. I have had my time with kings
drinking mead and wine;

23. Awhile with kings unthinking,
mead and wine were we drinking;

*Following a suggestion in *EIL* glossary

today I drink whey and water
among withered hags.

24. May a little cup of whey be my ale;
    may all that annoys me be God's will;
    praying to Thee, O living God,
    may I set my body's ward against anger.

25. I see on my cloak spotted age;
    my mind begins deceiving me;
    the hair that grows through my skin is
        gray;
    like lichen on an old tree.

26. My right eye is taken from me
    to be sold for a land owned forever
        absolutely;
    and the left eye has been taken
    to make sure of the claim.

[27. Three floods
    that used to come from the high fort of
        Ruide:
    a flood of warriors, a flood of horses,
    a flood of greyhounds of the sons of
        Lugaid.]

28. Wave of the flood-tide
    and the excellent ebb:
    what the flood-wave gives you,
    the ebbing wave takes out of your hand.

29. The flood-wave
    and the second the ebb:
    all have come to me
    so that I know how to recognize them.

30. The flood-wave,
    may it not come to the silence of my
        chamber!
    though great my company in darkness,
    a hand was laid on them all.

31. Well might Mary's Son spend the night
    so that He was beneath the roof-pole of
        my chamber;
    though I offered no other hospitality,
    I said 'No' to no one.

today but whey and water
with women withered, shrinking.

24. Be a cup of whey my ale;
    what vexes, ay be God's will.
    God, I pray in my behalf
    let not wrath my body fill.

25. Clotted cloak of age on me;
    my sense deceives me surely;
    gray the hair grows through my skin
    as on old trees the lichen.

26. My right eye taken away,
    sold for land, mine alway;
    the left eye taken surely
    to clench the claim utterly.

[27. Thrice flooding
    from Ruide's high fort running:
    flood of horses, flood of men,
    flood of hounds, Lugaid's
        huntsmen.]

28. Wave flooding
    and swift ebb along the land;
    what full flood waves bring to you,
    ebb waves carry from your hand.

29. Wave flooding
    and the second wave ebbing
    have come to me, not sudden,
    I know their tangled webbing.

30. Wave flooding
    comes not to chamber studding;
    my company, though ample,
    on all a hand fell thudding.

31. Well might lodge Mary Mother
    or Christ within my chamber;
    though I offered no other
    cheer, I denied no stranger.

32. Pity everyone
    (man is the least free of creatures)
    whose ebb was not seen
    as his flood had been.

33. My flood;
    it is well my loan was preserved.
    Jesus, Mary's Son, saved it
    so that I am not sad at ebb.

34. Well for the island of the great sea:
    flood comes to it after the ebb;
    as for me, I expect no flood
    after the ebb.

35. Hardly a house today
    I could recognize;
    what was once in flood
    is now all ebb.

32. Woe to all!
    Of creatures man is most small;
        his floodtide was seen flowing,
    but unseen his ebbtide's fall.

33. My flooding
        kept well my loan from spending.
    Christ helped me hoard in heaven;
        not sad am I at ebbing.

34. Happy isle in the great sea:
    flood after ebb comes duly;
        I think no more will fate bring
    flood to me after ebbing.

35. Scarce a house I know today,
        hut or shelter or steading;
    what was once in prime budding,
        then flooding, now all ebbing.
            Ebbing.

Meter: The meter changes with almost every stanza (see below). The popularity of the poem—as the many versions of it suggest—led to accretion, as in the instance of st 27, which is st 1 of no. 78 and doesn't really belong in this poem at all. St 16 is similarly probably an import, although I know of no other poem to attribute it to.

St 1, $7_2 7_1 7_1 7_2$; rime 2/4.
Stt 2, 13–15, 19, 25–26, *deibide*; stt 14 and 19, rhythmic rimes 1/2.
St 3, $3_2 7_2 7_3 7_3$; *deibide* with rhythmic rimes.
Stt 4, 8, 9, 11, 16, 21, 31, $7_2$ throughout; rime 2/4 in all these, line 1 consonating in stt 8, 9, 16; rime 1/3 in stt 11 and 21; linking rime 3/4 in stt 8, 9, 16; internal rime 3/4 in st 11.
St 5, $7_3 7_2 7_3 7_2$; rime 1/3, 2/4.
St 6, $3_1 7_1 7_1 7_1$; rime 1/2/4; linking rime 3/4.
St 7, $7_2 7_2 7_1 7_2$; rime 1/2/4; linking rime 3/4.
St 10, $7_3 7_3 7_1 7_3$; rime 1/2/4; linking rime 3/4.
St 12, $3_1 7_1 7_2 7_3$; *deibide* with rhythmic rimes 1/2.
St 17, $3_1 7_1 7_1 7_2$; *deibide*.
St 18, $3_1 7_1 7_1 7_1$; *deibide* with rhythmic rimes.
Stt 20, 24, $7_1$ throughout; rime 2/4, linking rime 3/4; st 24 only, internal rime 1/2.
St 22, $7_1 7_3 7_2 7_3$; rime 2/4; linking rime 3/4.
St 23, $7_1 7_2 7_3 7_2$; rime 1/2/4; linking assonance 3/4.
St 28, $3_2 7_1 7_1 7_1$; rime 2/4.
Stt 29–30, 33, $3_2 7_2 7_2 7_2$; st 29 and 33, rime 1/3, 2/4; st 30, rime 1/2/4, internal rime 3/4.
St 32, $3_2 7_2 7_3 7_2$; rime 1/2/4.
St 34, $7_1 7_1 7_1 7_2$; *deibide* with rhythmic rime 1/2.
St 35, $7_1 7_2 7_2 7_2$; rime 2/4; linking rime 3/4.

# { 47 }
# Liadan Loses Cuirithir
*Cen áinius*

The story of Liadan and Cuirithir comes to us as a handful of poems with the sketch of a story in prose. The two were lovers. They are separated and Liadan takes the veil. Cuirithir, who was a poet, follows her by taking orders also. He especially finds it difficult to keep his vows. At one point they subject themselves to St. Cuimine, who, when he feels they are ready, tests them by letting them sleep together in the presence of a young boy. They fail this test and Cuirithir is banished. The lament here is uttered by Liadan.

1. Without joy
   the deed that I have done:
   what I loved, I troubled.

2. It were madness
   not to do his pleasure,
   except for fear of the King of Heaven.

3. It were no loss
   for him, the meeting he desired,
   seeking Paradise through pain.

4. Small worth
   what troubled Cuirithir about me;
   my gentleness toward him was great.

5. I am Liadan;
   I loved Cuirithir;
   it is true as is said.

6. A short while
   I was in Cuirithir's company;
   my companionship was good toward him.

7. Music of the woods
   used to sing to me with Cuirithir,
   with the voice of the deep red sea.

8. I would have thought
   Cuirithir would not have been troubled
   by any meeting I made.

9. Do not conceal it;
   he was my heart's true love,
   though I loved everyone besides.

1. No pleasure
   in deed done to loving-one;
   tormenting without measure.

2. What madness
   not to give him happiness,
   though fear of God feed sadness.

3. No ruin,
   his affair desirable
   through pain heaven pursuing.

4. Cause slender
   through me troubled Cuirithir,
   though I was gentle, tender.

5. I'm Liadan;
   it is I loved Cuirithir,
   truly, though said by heathen.

6. Brief hour
   together with Cuirithir;
   our closeness then a dower.

7. Woods singing
   to me beside Cuirithir
   with somber sea-sounds dinning.

8. I wonder
   it would trouble Cuirithir,
   any deal made asunder.

9. No hiding:
   he was my heart's true-lover,
   though I loved all beside him.

10. A roar of fire
    has broken my heart;
    it is known that without him I cannot
        live.

      Meter: 3₂7₃7₂; rime 1/3.

10. Flames flowing
    burst my heart, now desperate,
    dead without him—this knowing. No.

## { 48 }

# Eve

*Mé Éba, ben Adaim uill*

1. I am Eve, wife of great Adam;
   it is I who did Jesus wrong in the past;
   it is I who stole heaven from my children;
   it is I who should have gone on the tree.

2. I had a royal house to my desire;
   evil the bad choice that disgraced me;
   evil the reproving of the crime that has
       withered me;
   alas! my hand is not clean.

3. It is I who took the apple from above;
   my gluttony went beyond my powers;
   as long as they live with day
   women will not give up folly.

4. There would be no ice anywhere;
   there would be no bright winter of
       great winds;
   there would be no hell; there would be
       no grief;
   there would be no fear, if it were not
       for me.

1. Me? Adam's wife, Eve I am.
       Jesus saddens at my wrong.
   I stole heaven from my kin;
       I by right the rood were on.

2. Once a palace I controlled;
       by malice of choice demeaned;
   harsh blow hinders; I am blamed;
       my shamed fingers never cleaned.

3. I ate that apple, sweet food,
       in the grapple of great greed;
   while we're living under sky
       women and I folly breed.

4. Nowhere simply cold and snow;
       no wild wintry winds would be,
   no Hell, no sorrow nor moan,
       no groan of fear—but for me! Me.

    Meter: 7₁ throughout; rime 3/4; each stanza has either long or short vowels throughout and line 1 consonates with 2/4; internal rime between 1/2 (imperfect in st 2); stt 2 and 3, linking rime 3/4; stt 1 and 2, all lines consonate.

## { 49 }

# Little Jesus
*Ísucán*

As St. Brigit became confused in the Irish mind with the Virgin (no. 32), St. Ite in her devotion thought that the Infant Jesus came to her to be nursed and that miraculously she was able to feed Him. Lives of her add this poem in margins of manuscripts, much as the Old English Caedmon's Hymn is added even in Latin lives like Bede's that paraphrase the poem in Latin.

1. [It is] little Jesus
  Who is nursed by me in my little
    hermitage:
  though a cleric is with great treasure
  it is all a lie but little Jesus.

1. Jesukin,
  I nurse Thee past reasoning:
  though cleric win the great prize,
  all is lies but Jesukin.

2. Nursing that is nursed by me in my
    house
  is not fosterage of a low-born churl;
  Jesus with men of heaven
  is against my heart every single night.

2. The nursing I do at home
  is no base churl's fostering;
  Jesus and hosts redeeming
  evenings I clutch prospering.

3. Little young Jesus [is] my lasting good:
  He gives and is not remiss;
  the King Who rules all,
  not to pray to Him, that will bring
    regret.

3. Jesus my good ay making,
  He gives it unforgetting;
  King, Ruler, all obeying,
  no praying, then regretting.

4. Noble Jesus of angels
  is not an ordinary cleric
  that is nursed by me in my little
    hermitage,
  Jesus, Son of the Hebrew woman.

4. Just Jesus of Cherubim,
  no mean cleric, foolish one,
  I nurse Thee while worshipping,
  Jesus of the Jewish one.

5. Sons of princes, sons of kings,
  into my land though they come;
  not from them do I expect advantage;
  I prefer little Jesus.

5. Sons of princes, sons of kings
  toward rings of land issuing,
  not theirs the gain I burn for,
  I yearn for thee, Jesukin

6. Sing a chorus, maidens.
  to the Man Who deserves your small
    assessment:
  He is in that port above
  though on my lap is little Jesus.

6. Maidens, hail by hymning Him,
  your tribute of fees to Him;
  He is above visiting
  though at my heart, Jesukin.
  Jesukin.

Meter: st 1, $3_3 7_3 7_1 7_3$, rime 1/2/4; stt 2 and 5, $7_1 7_3 7_2 7_3$, rime 2/4, linking rime 3/4; st 5 only, linking rime 1/2; st 3, $7_2$ throughout, rime 2/4, consonance 1/2/4; stt 4 and 6, $7_3$ throughout, rime 2/4; st 4, consonance 1/2/4; st 6, consonance 2/3/4.

## [ 50 ]
# Lament for Dinertach
*It é saigte gona súain*

The speaker is either wife or daughter of Guaire, King of Aidne in Con-
naught. He was noted for his generosity and appears also in nos. 43 and
44. Dinertach's father, also named Guaire, was not a king and came from
northern Munster. Dinertach was probably killed aiding the Connaught
King Guaire, who was defeated in the Battle of Carn Conaill in 649 by the
King of Ireland. King Guaire had been trying to take over part of north-
ern Munster.

1. These are the arrows that slay sleep
   every hour in the cold night:
   loveshafts from his companionship after
      day
   of the man from beside the land of
      Roigne.

2. Too much love for the man of another
      country
   who excelled his contemporaries
   has taken my looks, not enough color
      remains;
   it does not let me sleep.

3. Sorrowful
   that I did not see Dinertach;
   around the son of Guaire son of
      Nechtain,
   around him would be no danger.

4. Sweeter than songs was his speech—
   except for the holy worship of the King
      of heaven—
   a splendid flame without boasting,
   a slender, soft-sided mate.

5. When I was a child I was modest;
   I used not to go to evil trysts;
   since I came to the uncertainty of age,
   my wantonness has led me astray.

6. I have every good with Guaire,
   with the king of cold Aidne;
   my mind wishes to go from my people
   into the land in Irluachair.

1. These darts slay sleep, all rest gone,
   through every numb hour, nightlong;
      love pangs from num'rous nights
         spent
      with one from Roigne pleasant.

2. Great love for a foreign lad,
   better than any comrade,
      took my beauty, paled my cheek,
      allows me no more sound sleep.

3. Dinertach,
   woe he was unseen ere that
      'round him danger should threaten,
      'round Guaire's son O'Nechtan.

4. Sweeter than song his speaking,
   except God's hymns, heav'n-seeking;
      fierce flame without boast or pride,
      a slender spouse with soft side.

5. No evil tryst broke my rest
   when I was young and modest;
      grown to greater years, more free,
      my wanton ways deceive me.

6. With Guaire I find all well,
   king of cold Aidne, able;
      but my thoughts would go flying
      to Irluachair outlying.

7.  In the land of lovely Aidne,
    about Cell Colman there is singing
       of the fair flame from south of Limerick
          of the tombs,
    of him whose name is Dinertach.

7.  They sing in old Aidne well
    around calm Colman's chapel
       of Dinertach, fierce flame stirred
       from Limerick, grave-covered.

8.  My heavy heart is tortured,
    Holy Christ, by his murder:
    these are the arrows that slay sleep
    every hour in the cold night.

8.  Holy Christ, my heart is rent;
    his murder is my torment:
       these darts slay sleep, all rest gone,
       through every numb hour,
          nightlong.

Meter: *deibide*; st 3 has rhythmic rimes and the first line is shortened: $3_3 7_3 7_2 7_2$. I suspect this stanza was taken from some other poem on Dinertach. Meyer and Murphy do not translate it; Greene and O'Connor emend to get an unlikely first two lines with two trisyllabic rime words in each, separated only by a one-syllable particle.

# { 51 }
## The Sweetheart
### *Cride é*

He is (my) heart,
an acorn,
he is a dear boy,
a kiss for him.

Heart is he,
   nut of oaks;
brisk is he,
   kissed one dotes.

Meter: $3_1$ throughout; rime 1/3, 2/4 consonating; internal rime 3/4.

# { 52 }
## A Girl Sings
### *Gel cech núa—sásad nglé!*

Everything new is bright—fully
   satisfying!
The behavior of young people is
   changeable;
beautiful are judgments concerning
   love;
sweet are the words of a man courting.

Dear each new thing, never dull;
young folks' wishes are fickle;
   fair the choices love can bring;
   sweet the words of youth wooing.

Meter: *deibide*.

# { 53 }

# Loveloneliness †

*Och is fada atáim a-muigh*

This poem is probably the most recent in the collection. The speaker has been deserted by her lover, and realizes that he has always meant more to her than she to him. But she has also heard a rumor that he has deserted her for a man. She is reluctant to accept this, but at last admits that whoever may have lured him from her, she is nevertheless alone.

1. Alas, it is long that I am away
   from the person on whom is my love;
   though it serve as a judgment,
   each day seems longer to me than to
      him.

1. Woe, I am away too long
   from one I love, gone is he;
   though it serve as fate this way,
   each day seems longer to me.

2. Around him I am not cheerless,
   although his smile on me does not last;
   two stories I will not accept:
   if he be a woman, if she be a man.

2. With him I'm not without cheer,
   though his smiles here briefly hang;
   two stories go not with me:
   be he woman, be she man.

3. I am my comrade forever;
   I shall not give love by right;
   although it be she or though it be he,
   Alas, O God! alas, alas.

3. I am my comrade till doom.
   I'll not have room to love so;
   though it were she or were he,
   pity me, God, ochone, woe! Woe!

Meter: 7, throughout; 2.4 defective.

# Miscellaneous Poems

## { 54 }
## Cat and Scholar
*Messe ocus Pangur bán*

1. I and white Pangur,
   each of us at his special skill:
   his mind is on hunting,
   my own mind on my special craft.

2. I love quiet better than any fame,
   with my book in diligent study;
   white Pangur does not envy me:
   he loves his childish skill.

3. A tale without boredom when we
   are at home, the two of us alone,
   we have boundless sport,
   something to which we devote our
       ingenuity.

4. Frequently after valorous fights
   a mouse sticks in his net;
   as for me, into my net falls
   a difficult rule hard to understand.

5. Against a hedge wall he points
   his bright perfect eye;
   I point my own against the keenness of
       science,
   my clear eye, though weak.

6. He rejoices with a quick motion
   when a mouse sticks in his sharp claw;
   when I understand a precious, hard
       problem
   I too rejoice.

1. Pangur Ban and I, each bent
   on using his own talent:
       his heart on hunting will be,
       mine on my special study.

2. Better than fame is knowing,
   my book freely following:
       Pangur envies not my wish;
       he loves his chores, though childish.

3. Two at home, not bored are we,
   together ever happy;
       each one doing his own thing,
       his special skill pursuing.

4. After brave battles occur,
   his net may a mouse capture;
       in my own net falls as well
       a rough rule in sense subtle.

5. His clear acute eye he sets
   fixed on the fence-wall complex;
       I, my own eye, weak yet bright,
       I bring to bear on insight.

6. He is glad to move quickly
   with mouse caught in paw-prickly;
       I too am glad when I plumb
       some dear difficult question.

7. Though we may be thus awhile
   neither bothers the other:
   each of us likes his art
   separately delighting in them.

7. Though for some time thus we are,
   each troubles not the other,
      good each thinks his craft to be,
      amusing himself only.

8. He is himself master of it,
   the work he does every single day;
   bringing the difficult to clarity
   is my own work.

8. Every day he does his work
   in which himself is expert;
      hard words I make clear and sure;
      I, too, work well like Pangur. Pangur.

Meter: *deibide*.

# [ 55 ]
# "What, All My Pretty Chickens?"
*Cumthach labras in lonsa*

1. Sorrowfully the blackbird speaks;
   the evil met with I know;
   he who took apart his house
   slaughtered his birds.

1. Mournful music—blackbird's call:
   I know the deed done, fatal;
      he who hacked his home went then
      and wracked to death his children.

2. The evil that happened to him now
   not long ago I met with;
   good is my recognition of your speech,
      O blackbird,
   after your house was destroyed.

2. The ill he's now incurring
   lately I was suffering.
      Well his cry is known to me,
      last farewell to home, wholly.

3. Your heart, O blackbird, burns
   at what the unbridled fellow did:
   your nest without bird and without egg,
   a little matter for the cowherd.

3. Your heart, blackbird, burned and dulled
   by deeds of one unbridled;
      there your nest—no egg, no bird—
      no care expressed by cowherd.

4. They used to come to your clear voice
   your new household hither;
   a bird does not come from your house,
   across the opening of your nest are
      nettles.

4. Once your young ones used to come
   when your clear call would summon;
      no more bird heeds and will wing;
      across your door weeds growing.

5. The herdsmen for cattle killed
   all your children in one single day;
   the same experience for me and for you,
   my children live no more.

5. They killed them and went away,
   those cowherds—all in one day;
      your mood and mine are the same:
      each child they slew, our heartpain.

6. She was feeding until evening,
   the mate [*lit.*, half-bird] of the foreign
   bird,

6. The blackbird's mate went in flight
   to feed in fields till twilight,

she went into the snare after that,
and found death from the cowherd.

but went into a snare then,
there to be rent by herdsmen.

7. O Man Who made the world,
   grievous to us your injustice;
   friends that are about us,
   their wives and sons are living.

7. Man Who made earth, have pity!
   Sad your partiality;
      friends have lives and comrades kin,
      men's sons and wives yet living.

8. The fairy host came with a rush
   to kill our households;
   it is a danger, though they were not
      taken by wounding;
   not worse their slaughter by weapons.

8. Fairy folk swooped with a whir
   on our people with slaughter;
      a curse, though no wounding come,
      not worse, their death by weapon.

9. Grief for wife, grief for children
   strong the care on us;
   without their going in and out
   my heart is full of grief.

9. Griefs for wife, for child stir me,
   strong the sorrow over me;
      in nor out they go—heart full
   I think about them mournful.
   Mournful.

Meter: *deibide* with much alliteration and internal rime 3/4, often with more than one word involved.

## { 56 }
# The Viking Threat
*Is aicher in gáeth in-nocht*

The wind tonight is bitter,
it tousles the sea's white hair;
I have no fear that gentle seas
will bring fierce warriors from Norway

Bitter is the wind tonight;
it flings the froth-sea foam-white;
   no fear soothing seas today
   speed wild warriors of Norway.

Meter: *deibide*.

## { 57 }
# A Splendid Sword †
*Luin oc elaib*

Blackbirds to swans,
ounces to heavy weights,
forms of common women
to splendid queens,
kings to Domnall,
a drone to choral music,
a rushlight to a candle:
swords to my sword.

Wren to eagle,
ounce to quintal,
coarse peasant women
to crowned queens simple,
czars to Domnall,
drone to clamor,
candle to gleaming:
glaives—my glaive's glamor.

Meter: 4₂4₂5₂5₂ with linking alliteration; rime 2/4, 6/8. Treated by James Carney as accentual like no. 15.

## [ 58 ]
## The Necessity of Reading †
### *Cid glic fri hailchi úara*

Though one be clever at cold splinters
    of rock,
though one be a master at handling an
    axe,
though his voice is sweet in singing,
I have heard that he who does not read
    is ignorant.

Though striking stones he's cunning,
    though wielding axe he's leading,
though sweet his song and humming,
    I hear he's dull, not reading.

Meter: 7₂ throughout; rime 1/3, 2/4.

## [ 59 ]
## You See Your Own Faults in Others †
### *Cid becc—mét friget—do locht*

Though your fault be small—the size
    of a nit
you notice it on anyone from a distance
though your fault be as big as a
    mountain,
you do not notice it on yourself.

You see on others afar
    your fault, though small as a mite;
you see your own not at all,
    though great as a mountain height.

Meter: 7₁ throughout; rime 1/3, 2/4.

## [ 60 ]
## Broad-minded Etan
### *Ní fetar*

I do not know
with whom Etan will sleep;
but I know that Etan the white
will not sleep alone.

I don't know
who'll be Etan's bedfellow,
    but I know Etan won't be
    sleeping alone and lonely.

Meter: *deibide* with shortened first line; rhythmic rimes 1/2; all final consonants consonate.

# { 61 }
## Satire on a Rustic
### Atá ben as-tír

There is a woman from the country,
I do not speak her name;
her fart breaks out of her
like a stone from a sling.

She's a rustic sort
   (her name I speak not)—
farts break from her gut
   like rocks a sling shot.

Meter: 5, throughout; rime 2/4; limited consonance throughout of line-endings, perfect 2/3/4.

# From the Sagas

## [ 62 ]

## Midir Summons Etain to Fairyland
*A bé find, in rega lim*

*The Wooing of Etain (Tochmarc Étaíne)* belongs to the Mythological Cycle. The story is especially interesting in the glimpses it gives of early beliefs and customs. Etain (Midir's second wife) passes through many shapes, transformed by Midir's first wife. Multiple marriages are regulated in the ancient laws, but these are characters from fairyland. Born again, Etain remembers nothing of her former existence but marries the king, Eochaid Airem. Midir returns from the Otherworld to claim her. He plays chess with the king, fulfilling all the demands of Eochaid with the aid of fairy helpers, and refusing to name his stake until he wins. In the final game, Midir wins and asks a kiss from Etain as the stake. When he embraces her, they turn to swans and vanish through the smoke-hole of the house. The poem is added to the third version of the tale, where it is inserted when Midir meets Etain before the chess game.

1. Fair lady, will you go with me
   into the land of wonder where there are
      stars?
   Hair there is like the crown of primroses
   and to its very tip the body is like snow.

1. Woman Fair, to lands aglow
   with magic stars wilt thou go?
      Primrose petals, hair in hue,
   and bodies there are like snow.

2. Neither mine nor thine exist there;
   teeth there are bright; eyebrows black;
   the number of our hosts there is a
      delight to the eye;
   each cheek there is the color of the
      foxglove.

2. There is neither mine nor thine;
   brows are black there, bright teeth
      shine;
      fair to see our hosts are spread;
   each cheek there glows foxglove red.

3. Every bog is the purple of the plain;
   eggs of blackbirds are a delight to the eye;
   though the sight of the Plain of Ireland
      is beautiful,
   it is lonely after the companionship of
      the Great Plain.

3. Purple plain is every moor;
   fair to see are merle's eggs pure;
      Eire was a lovely sight—
   lonely, since Great Plain's delight.

4. Though the ale of Ireland seems
      intoxication to you,
   ale of the Great Land is more
      intoxicating;
   a splendid land is the land I speak of;
   the young do not go [to death] before
      the old.

4. Though heady seems Ireland's beer,
   more heady the Great Land's here;
      grand the land of which I told;
      young die not before the old.

5. Gentle sweet streams [flow] across the
      land,
   choice mead and wine;
   noble, without flaw [are] the people;
   conception [is] without sin or guilt.

5. Sweet streams flow for earth, and then
      choice mead and wine there for men;
      fine perfect people there breathe,
      sinless, guiltless they conceive.

6. We see everyone on every side,
   and no one sees us;
   the darkness of Adam's sin
   hides us from being counted.

6. Everyone we see each way
      and none see us: dark of day
         from sin of Adam mounting
      hides us from any counting.

7. Woman, if you come to my vigorous
      people,
   a golden crown will be on your head;
   fresh pork, ale, milk and drink
   you will have with me there, Fair Lady.

7. Woman, if thou come with me,
   crown of gold we'll give to thee;
      fresh pork, ale, and milk prepare
      as thine with me, woman fair.
         Woman fair.

Meter: st 1, 7, throughout; rime 1/2/4; internal rime 1/2, 3/4; all lines conso-
nate; the rest of the poem is *deibide* with monosyllabic end words in rimed coup-
lets. The last stanza has all four lines riming.

[ 63 ]

# Fann's Farewell to Cu Chulainn †
*Fégaid mac láechraidi Lir*

*The Sickbed of Cu Chulainn or the Only Jealousy of Emir (Serglige Con Culainn
ocus Óenét Emire)* is a confusion of versions. Cu Chulainn's wife is some-
times Eithne, sometimes Emir. When Yeats used the characters, he took
the jealousy to be between these two. The tale is rather, like no. 62, a tale
of an Otherworld lover. Fann is the wife of Manannan mac Lir, an impor-
tant seagod for whom the Isle of Man is named. But Fann falls in love
with Cu Chulainn and, after letting him lie ill for a year, summons him to
the Otherworld. Cu Chulainn delays by sending his charioteer, Loeg, but
at last is persuaded to go to help one of the fairy kings against his enemies.
Emir tries to kill Fann, but Fann at last gives up her lover. This poem is
her renunciation. Yet Manannan must shake his cloak between the lovers
before they can forget each other and return willingly to their own mates.

1. See the champion son of Ler
   from the plains of Eogan Inbir:
   Manannan above the world of hills,
   there was a time he was dear to me.

2. Today my cry would be keen;
   my proud spirit does not love him:
   vain is the matter of love:
   knowledge of it goes without delay.

3. The day the son of Ler and I were
          together
   in the sun-house of Dun Inbir,
   it seemed likely to us without a stay
   that there should be no separation from
          each other.

4. When fine Manannan took me,
   I was a fitting mate:
   he could not take from me at the time
   an extra game of chess.

5. When fine Manannan took me,
   I was a fitting mate:
   the bracelet of gold that I have
   he gave me as the price of my blushes.

6. Out across the heath I had
   fifty maidens in many colors:
   I gave him fifty men
   besides the fifty maidens.

7. Four times fifty without mistake:
   that is the household in a single house;
   twice fifty prosperous healthy men,
   twice fifty fair wholesome women.

8. I see here across the sea—
   no one confused sees him—
   the horseman of the long-haired sea;
   he does not keep to the longships.

9. At your going past us up to now
   none but a fairy sees:
   your senses magnify every fine
          company,
   although they are distant from you.

---

1. See the warrior son of Ler
   from plains of Eogan Inbir:
       Manannan mounts the world's hill;
       his love once my heart would fill.

2. Today my cry would be sharp;
   no love lies in heavy heart;
       for love is a vain affair,
       quickly fading everywhere.

3. When I and Mac Lir, my spouse,
   shared Dun Inbir's bright sunhouse,
       we thought no moment would bring
       to him and me a parting.

4. When Manannan married me,
   I, a fitting mate, surely,
       he would try to win in vain
       from me once the odd chess game.

5. When Manannan married me,
   I, a fitting mate, surely:
       my golden bracelet he says
       paid the price of my blushes.

6. I had far across the moors
   fifty girls in bright colors;
       I gave him, too, fifty men
       besides the maidens given.

7. Four times fifty—no mistake—
   folk of one house as keepsake:
       a hundred women, fair, fit,
       a hundred men, fine fortunate.

8. O'er the sea I watch him come;
   none mad sees aught on ocean;
       horseman on heaving seas sits,
       not following on longships.

9. Until now your going past
   just fairies saw by contrast;
       large each small host to your sense,
       though far away in distance.

10. As for me, it is fitting for me,
      because the wits of women are foolish:
          he whom I greatly love
          has brought me here into trouble.

11. Farewell to you, fair Cu!
      Behold, we go from you proudly;
          that I were not going is our wish:
      every rule is noble until it is
          transgressed.

12. It is time for me to go:
      there is someone with whom it is
          difficult:
      the distress is great indeed,
      Loeg, son of Riangabra.

13. I shall go with my own mate,
      because he will not do what I do not
          wish;
      you may not say it is proceeding in
          secret:
      if it please you, look.

10. I found it fitting and just—
      for women are not to trust—
          he whom I loved beyond all
          has brought about my downfall.

11. Farewell, kind Cu, here abide;
      I go from thee in high-pride.
          Parting wish is left undone:
          good every rule till broken.

12. It is time for me to go;
      one finds it hard—that I know;
          great indeed the loss I fear,
          O Loeg, son of Riangabir.

13. I shall go with my own mate:
      he breaks not my will, my fate.
          Do not say in stealth I flee:
          watch if you will; let all see. See.

Meter: *deibide* with one pair of rhythmic rimes each in stt 1, 2, 10, and 12.

# [ 64–68 ]
# Poems Attributed to Suibne the Madman

According to the legend, Suibne (Sweeney), a king in the far north of Ireland, was driven mad by the cries at the battle of Mag Rath (or by the curse of St. Ronan). He lived in trees, grew feathers and talons, and shunned mankind. At last, befriended by the saint Mo Ling, he turned from his wild ways, and at his death the saint gave him Christian burial. The reference to Mo Ling at the end of the first poem here may have led to its being assigned to Suibne. Like Kenneth Jackson, I believe that the poem "God's House" (no. 27) is probably a hermit poem that has been incorrectly attributed to Suibne because of the reference to "points" (Suibne was to die by a point). But Suibne constantly complains of homelessness in his madness, so that there seems no more reason for accepting "God's House" as his than some of those attributed to Finn that I have also rejected.

Poem no. 64 seems to be about the river Garb. The language suggests the poem is not earlier than the twelfth century. Suibne lived in the seventh century. But inasmuch as we cannot be sure any of the poems were actually composed by Suibne, I have placed this one here. Poems 65–68 are from the *Buile Suibne* ("The Frenzy of Suibne"), and some of the poems in this tale are also no earlier than the twelfth century, like the prose that seems to have been added to give a setting for the poems. We learn in several different sources that the importance of Suibne's madness is the collection of poems that he composed. These poems are all in the spirit of that collection.

## [ 64 ]
# The Cry of the Sweetsounding Garb
### *Gáir na Gairbe glaídbinne*

1. The cry of the sweetsounding Garb
   that roars against the beginning wave!
   Vast delightful shoals
   of fish swimming about in its breast.

2. My patience seems short to me,
   watching floodtides that fill the banks,
   the strong surge of the great Garb,
   water throwing it back.

3. Pleasant it is when they struggle with
      each other,
   floodtide and ebbtide chilly;
   in succession they occur
   downward and from below, continually.

4. A strain of music that I hear
   in the Garb with the brightness of
      winter;
   during great boisterousness I sleep
   in the cold icy night.

5. Shorebirds with music,
   sweet tunes are their customary cries;
   concerning them nostalgia has seized me
   as they celebrate the hours.

6 Sweet to me is the ousel's whistling
   and hearing mass;
   my stay seems short to me
   on the height above Durad Faithlenn.

7. It is to those tunes that I sleep
   on peaks and on branches;
   the music that I hear
   is minstrelsy for my soul.

1. The calling Garb, sweetsounding
      roars at the billows brimming;
   great gorgeous schools, deepsounding,
      embracing fish there swimming.

2. Brief seems my passivity,
      watching floods fill the courses:
   great Garb's grand activity
      tossed back by water forces.

3. Splendid their wild grappling,
      floodtide and ebbtide chilling,
   up—down, in turn battling,
      emptying, then refilling.

4. I hear sweet tunes singing out:
      Garb bound by winter whit'ning;
   I sleep, mad mirth ringing out
      at night, crisp, cold, calm,
         fright'ning.

5. Shorebirds ever wailing there,
      song-sweet their cries enchanting;
   lone longing assailing there,
      hearing each hour of chanting.

6. Bright the blackbird's whistling,
      murmur of mass and praying;
   brief seems my pause listening
      on Durad Faithlenn straying.

7. 'Midst all that I'm slumbering
      on hill-tops or on branches;
   music I hear wondering,
      my soul's delight enhances.

8. Music of psalms with psalm-purity
   at the point of Ros Bruic without
      permanence;
   the roar of the brown stag bellowing
   from the slope of cold Erc.

9. Very cold sleep of one night;
   hearing the stormy waves;
   widespread voices of birds
   from the thicket of Cuille Wood.

10. Moan of a wintry wind;
    sound of storm below an oak:
    the cold sheet of ice groans
    cracking at the cry of the Garb.

11. It is hard to attend canonical hours
    at which bells are struck without
       silence
    for the noise of Inber Douglas
    and the cry of the Garb.

12. The sea of the noisy ocean
    westward around the doors of Airbre—
    the shorter to me at my rest
    listening to the cry of the Garb.

13. Druim Lethet in abundance
    has brown acorns on its oaks;
    its echo is a wonder
    that answers with me the sound of the
       Garb.

14. The falls of Maige, the falls of
       Dubthaige,
    Assaroe to which salmon run,
    though many are its stories,
    sweeter is the voice of the Garb.

15. Benn Boirche, Benn Bogaine
    and Glen Bolcain in silence;
    many nights, many evenings
    I have come at the sound of the Garb.

16. The Bay of Tuaige, Bay of Rudraige
    (their heights are not close):
    shorter to me than watching them
    is listening to the sound of the Garb.

8. Music of psalms, mellowing,
      by Ros Bruic, soon named Mullin;
   roar of red stags bellowing
      where slopes cold Erc, the sullen.

9. Sleep of one night, deep chilling,
      hearing high breakers pounding,
   great groups of birds shriek shrilling
      from Cuilenn Wood around 'em.

10. Winter winds wail battering
       under oaks, storm is moaning;
    cold sheets of ice crackling,
       burst by the great Garb's groaning.

11. Hard to hear hours beckoning
       with bells constantly sounding;
    Inber Dubglas echoing
       and the great Garb resounding.

12. Ocean currents weltering
       west 'round Airbre's gates curling;
    brief seems while I'm sheltering,
       hearing the great Garb skirling.

13. Druim Lethet rains steadily;
       acorns from oaktrees falling,
    its rich echo readily
       answers the great Garb calling.

14. Falls—Maige, Dubthach, Assaroe
       where run red salmon flashing,
    tales of you three mass enow,
       but Garb's voice is surpassing.

15. Bogain', Bolcan—silent one—
       and Mourne Mountains, north lying,
    nights and noons, Garb, strident one,
       calls me from you with crying.

16. Tuag, Rudraige glistening—
       waves far asunder swelling;
    shorter by Garb listening
       than watching those waves welling.

17. Strong watercourse of prophecy—
　　sweet is its high waterfall in beauty;
　　the Tacarda, angel-like—
　　what waterfall is purer of voice?

18. O affectionate Mo Ling
　　to whom I have brought the end of my
　　　　　game,
　　make my protection
　　against hell whose cry is rough.

17. Staunch stream foretold, stumbling,
　　tuneful voice, none is surer;
　　the Tacarda tumbling,
　　what cascade carols purer?

18. Loved Mo Ling accepting me,
　　with you my game ends stalling;
　　be ever protecting me
　　against hell's garbled calling.

Meter: 7₃7₂7₃7₂; rime 1/3, 2/4; considerable alliteration.

# [ 65 ]
# The Snow Is Cold Tonight†
### *In-nocht is fúar in snechta*

1. Tonight the snow is cold,
　　my poverty now is permanent,
　　I have no strength in the conflict,
　　I am a madman, wounded by hunger.

2. Everyone sees I am not shapely,
　　my rags are threadbare,
　　Suibne of Ros Ercain is my name,
　　the crazy madman I am.

3. I do not rest when night comes,
　　my foot approaches no path,
　　I shall not be here long,
　　the birdflocks of terror come toward me.

4. My goal is across the sea full of ships,
　　going over the ocean full of prows,
　　fear has seized my petty strength,
　　I am the mad one of Glen Bolcain.

5. The frosty wind rends me,
　　snow has wounded me as well,
　　the storm carries me off toward death
　　from the branches of every limb.

6. Green branches have wounded me,
　　they have torn my palms,
　　the briars have not left
　　the making of a girdle for my feet.

1. Tonight the snow is chilling,
　　filling my cup of sadness;
　　I have no strength for struggle,
　　at length in hungry madness.

2. All see I am not shapely,
　　my tatters hide me poorly:
　　I am Sweeney of Ros Ercain,
　　a madman am I, surely.

3. There comes no sleep with nighttime;
　　my feet can find no pathway;
　　I dare not wait here longer,
　　fear is stronger in halfday.

4. My aim: to sail out yonder,
　　crossing the fair main over;
　　but fear has sapped my courage;
　　I forage here, mad rover.

5. The frosty breezes rending,
　　and snow that freezes, blanches;
　　the storm has hurled me, flying,
　　dying, to earth from branches.

6. Brown branches wounding, cleaving,
　　my helpless hands are tearing;
　　the briars have stripped me leaving
　　no weaving for my wearing.

7. My hands are trembling,
   throughout all the earth there is cause
       of turmoil,
   from Slieve Mis to Slieve Cuillenn,
   from Slieve Cuillenn to Cooley.

7. My hands are trembling, shaking,
       all lands confuse us truly
   from Slieve Mis to Slieve Cuillenn,
       from Slieve Cuillenn to Cooley.

8. Forever sad is my cry
   on the mound of Cruachan Aighle,
   from Glen Bolcain to Islay,
   from Cenn Tire to Boirche.

8. Forever sad my wailing
       on top of Cruachan Oighle,
   from Glen Bolcain to Islay,
       from Kintire up to Boirche.

9. My share when day comes is small,
   it does not come as the new day's right,
   a crop of watercress of Luain Cille
   with cuckoo flower of Cell Cua.

9. Small my meal at day's dawning:
       it comes not as belonging:
   watercress of Luain Cille
       with cuckoo-flower joining.

10. As long as he is at Ros Ercach,
    trouble nor evil will come to him,
    what makes me without strength
    is being naked in snow.

10. At Ros Ercach no trouble
        nor distress there is rightful;
    my woe makes weakness double,
        naked in snow at nightfall. Tonight.

Meter: 7₂ throughout; rime 2/4; st 1, internal rime and linking rime 1/2, 3/4;
stt 2, 3, linking rime 3/4; internal rime 1/2, consonance 1/2, linking rime 3/4;
st 4, internal rime 1/2, 3/4, consonance and final syllables rime throughout,
linking rime 3/4; st 5, near rime 1/3, linking rime 3/4; st 6, consonance 1/3,
linking rime 3/4; st 7, internal rime 1/2, linking near rime 1/2, 3/4; st 8, inter-
nal rime 1/2, 3/4, assonance 1/2, linking rime 3/4; st 9, consonance 1/2, link-
ing rime 3/4; st 10, rime 1/3. Repetitions seem to count as internal and linking
rimes in some stanzas. The imitation catches only a few.

# [ 66 ]
# My Night in Cell Derfile †
### M'agaid i cCill Derffile

Dal Araide is in north Ireland, the land where Suibne was king. Faolchu,
in one story, is a son of Congal. Congal brought the forces of Scotland,
England, and Wales against the king Domnall, his foster father. He was
defeated and Suibne went mad at the Battle of Mag Rath.

1. My night in Cell Derfile,
   that it is that has broken my heart;
   sad for me, O my God's Son,
   parting from Dal Araide.

1. My night in Dervill's Chapel—
   my heart a broken chattel;
       Son of God, grief for me
   parting from Dal Araide.

2. Ten hundred and ten warriors,
   that was my army at Druim Fraoch;

2. Ten and ten hundred men stand
   at Druim Fraoch—they were my band;

although I am without strength, O Son
    of God,
it was I who was their chief in counsel.

God's Son! my strength is not well,
    though I was chief of counsel.

3. My night tonight is gloomy
without servant and without
    encampment;
not so was my night at Druim Dam,
I and Faolchu and Congal.

3. My night tonight gloomy, wan
without fort, without footman;
    not so my night with those two
    I with Congal and Faolchu.

4. Alas that I was kept back for the
    meeting,
O my Prince of the glorious kingdom,
though I should get no ill from it
forever but this one night.

4. Woe the meeting held me from
Christ, the Lord of Kingdom come!
    Though from that no hurt is mine
    forever but this nighttime.

Meter: *deibide* with several rhythmic rimes.


## [ 67 ]
# The Woman Who Reaps the Watercress†
*A ben benus a birar*

1. Woman who cuts the watercress
and who takes the water,
you would not be without anything
    tonight
though you did not take my meal.

1. O dame who takes the cresses
    and water in proportion,
you would need for naught tonight
    had you not plucked my portion.

2. Alas, little woman,
you will not go the way that I shall go,
I outside in the tree tops,
you over there in a friend's house.

2. Woe is me, O harridan,
    you go not where I'm heading;
out in tops of trees I am,
    you stand at a friend's steading.

3. Alas, little woman,
the wind that has come to me is cold;
mother nor son pities me;
there is no mantle on my neck.

3. Woe is me, O harridan,
    a cold wind past me sweeping;
son nor mother lends a hand;
    no rag my breast is keeping.

4. If you knew, little woman,
how Suibne is here,
both he gets no sympathy from anyone,
and no one gets his sympathy.

4. If you knew, O harridan,
    how Suibne here must linger;
none lifts a finger for him;
    for none lifts he a finger.

5. I do not go into an assembly
among warriors of my country;

5. I go not to a gathering
    with fellow warriors dauntless;

no safeguard is made me,
  my attention goes not with kingship.

6. I do not go as a guest
  to the house of anyone's son in Ireland;
  more often I have foolish madness
  on the pointed mountain peaks.

7. None comes to perform music for me
  for a while before going to bed;
  I get no sympathy
  from tribesman or kinsman.

8. When I was Suibne
  and used to go on horses,
  when that comes in my recollection
  alas that I remained alive.

9. I am Suibne, noble chief,
  my place is cold and unpleasant,
  though tonight I am on wild peaks,
  woman who takes my watercress.

10. My mead is my cold water,
  my cattle are my watercress,
  my friends are my trees,
  though I am without cloak, without
    shirt.

11. The night is cold tonight,
  though I am poor as regards watercress,
  I have heard the voice of the barnacle
    goose
  above bare Imleach of yewtrees.

12. I am without cloak, without shirt,
  the evil hour is long that followed me,
  I take flight at the cry of the crane
  as if it were a blow that hit me.

13. I reach the stronghold of Dairbre
  in the great days of spring,
  and I flee before night
  westward to Benn Boirche.

14. If you are experienced, white, wrinkled
    woman,
  my field is not active, hard and rough;

no safeguard mine, wandering,
  of kingship wholly thoughtless.

6. I do not go visiting
  in homes of men of Erin,
  but stray mad and shivering
  where mountain peaks are leering.

7. No one comes as sedative
  to sing a sleepy ditty;
  no tribesman, no relative
  will give me of his pity.

8. Once Suibne in verity,
  I on a steed, a rover—
  when that comes to memory,
  would that my life were over.

9. I am Suibne, high-hearted,
  chill woe my house oppresses,
  though I on peaks, sky-parted,
  O dame who takes my cresses.

10. The cold water is my wine,
  for kine I count my cresses;
  these are my comrades, my wood;
  me hood nor tunic dresses.

11. Cold tonight is the evening;
  my plight is poor in cresses;
  I heard a goose cry feeble,
  where Imlech Iobair stretches.

12. I without shirt or mantle—
  a long ill when they trailed me—
  I flee at cry of heron
  as though a felon flailed me.

13. I come to Dun of Dairbre
  in splendid spring awaking,
  and flee at evening restward,
  toward Boirche westward making.

14. If, cruel one, you are clever—
  my garth, a moor, a hollow—

there is one to whom it is a cause of
    sorrow,
the load you are carrying, wrinkled
    woman.

you bear away a burden,
    beldam, one sees in sorrow.

15. It is cold that they are
    on the edge of the clear sandy well,
    a bright draught of pure water
    and the watercress you cut.

15. Cold the drink from the wellspring
    on the brink of clean gravel,
    cold the bright water beaming
    and gleaming cress you gather.

16. My portion is the watercress you cut,
    the meal of a noble, thin madman;
    a cold wind springs about my loins
    from the peaks of every mountain.

16. My portion, cress you hoarded,
    a lean lord's crazy dining;
    chill blasts around my shoulder
    from colder mountains whining.

17. The morning wind is cold
    it comes between me and my shirt,
    I cannot speak to you,
    woman who cuts the watercress.

17. The dawn wind in jollity
    between shirt and me presses;
    we can hold no colloquy,
    O dame who takes the cresses.

WOMAN

18. Leave my meal to the Lord,
    be not hard on me;
    the more you will get leadership,
    and take a blessing, Suibne.

18. To God my goods deliver;
    let harshness then be hidden;
    bless you, and may you, Suibne,
    a speedy sway be given.

SUIBNE

19. Let us make a bargain, just and
    agreeable
    though I am on the top of a yew,
    take my shirt and my rags,
    leave the little bunch of watercress.

19. A bargain fair and fitting,
    though I on yew-top sitting:
    take shirt and ragged dresses,
    leave cresses for my picking.

20. There is hardly anyone to whom I am
    dear,
    my house is not on earth;
    since you take my watercress from me
    my share of sin be on your soul.

20. Scarce one now calls me lover;
    no craft on earth gives cover;
    since my cress you are craving,
    my failing be your trouble.

21. May you not reach the one whom you
    loved,
    the worse for him whom you followed;
    you have left one a poor man
    because of the bunch you cut.

21. Be your loved one forsaken—
    worse for him you tracked later—
    you left one poor humble,
    his bundle you have taken.

22. May a raid of the blue Norsemen take
    you,
    it was not a good meeting for me,

22. A raid of reavers seize you,
    misfortune mine to meet you;

may you get from the Lord the guilt
for cutting my meal of watercress.

for theft of cress may slander
and heaven's anger reach you.

23. Woman, if there should come to you
Loingsechan whose inclination is
    toward play,
give him through me a share:
half the watercress that you cut.

23. To Loingsechan, O woman,
give half the cress you ravage,
    from me the gift, a token
but broken without damage. O dame.

Meter: St 1 7₂7,7,7,7₂; rime 2/4.
Stt 2–4, 7,7₂7,7₂; rime 2/4; stt 2–3, linking rime 3/4; st 4, linking consonance 3/4.
Stt 5–9, 17, 7,7₂7,7₂; rime 1/3, 2/4 (rime 1/3 only approximate in st 7).
St 10, 7,7₂7,7₂; rime 2/4; linking rime 1/2; linking consonance, 3/4.
Stt 11–16, 18–23, 7₂ throughout; rime 2/4 in all these; st 19, rime 1/2/4; stt 12–16, 18–23, linking rime 3/4; stt 13–14, 16, internal rime 1/2; stt 18, 20–23, consonance 1/2.
The confusion of meters, the age of the language of different parts of the poem, and the repetition of phrases led to a reordering of stanzas discussed in *Etudes Celtiques* 7 (1956): 123–127.

## { 68 }
# Suibne on a Snowy Night
### Mór múich i túsa in-nocht

1. I am in great grief tonight,
   the clear wind has pierced my body,
   my feet are pierced, my cheek is gray,
   O great God! it is fitting for me.

1. Great grief tonight here I find;
       unkind wind wounded my form;
   my feet are pierced, pale my cheek.
       Great God, for bleak cause I mourn.

2. I was on Ben Boirche last night,
   the drops of cold Aughty beat me,
   tonight my limbs are broken
   in the hollow of a tree in bright Gaille.

2. I on Mourne mountains last night,
       drops would strike in Aughty cold;
   tonight my limbs, broken, blotched,
       in a notched tree in Gaille gold.

3. I have endured many a battle without
       weakness
   since down has grown on my body;
   every night and every day
   more and more I suffer ill.

3. I have withstood much stout strife
       since rife down rose on my skin;
   each dark, each day has its fill,
       more ill I suffer and sin.

4. Frost and unpleasant storm have
       tormented me,
   snow has beaten me on Slieve mic Sin;
   tonight the wind has wounded me,
   without the heather of safe Glen
       Bolcain.

4. Frost afflicts me, stormclouds black,
       on Kerry Stack stark snows beat;
   tonight winds wound me again,
       not Glen Bolcain's bracken sweet.

5. Fumbling is my shifting through every
       land,
   it has happened to me being without
       sense or reason,
   from Mag Line to Mag Li,
   from Mag Li to the wild Liffey.

6. I search across the forest of Slieve Fuait,
   in my course I reach Rathmore,
   across Mag Ai, across wild Mag Lorg
   I reach the corner of good Cruachan.

7. From Slieve Cua—no gentle journey—
   I reach clear Gaille stream;
   from Gaille stream, though a long step,
   I reach Slieve Breg in the east.

8. Miserable is the life, being without a
       house,
   sad is the life, O fair Christ!
   a satisfying crop of green-topped
       watercress,
   a drink of cold water from a clear brook.

9. Stumbling from the tops of withered
       branches,
   going through gorse—deed without a
       lie—
   avoiding people, in the company of
       wolves,
   racing red stags across a plain.

10. Sleeping at night without quilt in a wood
    on the top of a dense, bushy tree,
    without hearing voice nor noise,
    O Son of God, great is the misery.

11. Foolishly I run a course up a mountain-
        peak,
    alone, worn out because of activity;
    I have separated from my unblemished
        form,
    Son of God, great is the misery.

5. Restless I rove in each place,
       mine no grace of mind or sense;
   I pass Mag Line and Li,
       from Mag Li past Liffey thence.

6. Through Slieve Fuait forest I've found;
       I round Rathmore in my rush,
   across Mag Ai and Lorg Lonn,
       gone to Cruachan crest so lush.

7. From Slieve Cua (no ready run)
       I come by green Gaille's way
   from Gaille's glade (step that's steep)
       I come to song-sweet Slieve Brey.

8. Lone the life without a home;
       cruel the life, O Christ the kind,
   food—good crop of green-capped cress,
       drink from clear cold streams I find.

9. Fall from treetops of lank limbs,
       go through whins (true tales are told)
   away from men, walk with wolves,
       race red deer hooves on the wold.

10. Night spent in woods, naked, bare;
        treetops there are dense of leaf;
    not hearing sound or speech break:
        O Son of God, great the grief.

11. I rush 'round peaks, dazed with fright;
        few pass my flight (true belief);
    gone my faultless form and state:
        O Son of God, great the grief. Great
        grief.

Meter: 7₁ throughout; linking rime 3/4 throughout; linking rime 1/2, except in
st 8. The linking rime 1/2 in st 2 is doubtful; perhaps the consonance with all
four lines compensates.

## [ 69 ]
# The Cursed Banquet †
*In chuit sin chaithise in-nocht*

This poem comes from a story related to that of Suibne, in that it gives the
cause of the battle at Mag Rath, during which Suibne goes mad. This
poem is spoken by Gair Gann, a follower of Congal Claen (Crosseyed Con-
gal)—earlier called Congal Caech (Blind Congal)—urging him not to for-
give the insults that the King Domnall, whom Congal helped to the
throne, has put on him. Unknown to Domnall, the banquet was cursed
beforehand and Congal was the first to taste it.

1. "That meal that you eat tonight
   without pride, without purification:
   a hen's egg from the king you are not
       fond of
   and a goose egg to Maelodar.

1. "That meal, eaten without pride
   now unpurged, unpurified:
       hen egg from a king not dear
       but goose egg for Maelodar.

2. "I did not know before
   how noble was the king of the Oirgialla
   until I saw this Maelodar
   in the drinking hall receiving respect.

2. "Never knew I this before,
   Oirgiall's king with high honor,
       till I saw Maelodar come
       in winehall given welcome.

3. "If a single king without reproach
   had the territory of Conall and Eogan
   and the Oirgialla by act of spears
   he should not go into your place.

3. "If one king should own this all—
   lands of Eogan and Conall
       and Oirgiall by force and fear,
       your place he should not venture.

4. "That meal, though foreigners reject it,
   was given you in Domnall's house,"
   says Gair Gann, "may it not be
       wholesome for you
   if you eat the evil meal."

4. "That meal foreigners would shun
   you met in Domnall's mansion,"
       said Gair Gann, "for you no weal
       if you eat that evil meal."

Meter: *deibide*.

## [ 70–71 ]
# Ronan Kills His Son

Any story of an old king with a young wife who falls in love with his
attractive son will be compared with the Theseus-Hippolytus-Phaedra
tale. The son here is a great hunter, but not as devotee of Artemis, and
what hero is not hunter as well as warrior? The poems below are given in
the order of appearance in the manuscript; line numbers and text follow
David Greene's edition. Ronan's wife (referred to only as Eochaid's daugh-
ter) gives the first two lines of the first quatrain below; the son (Mael

Fothartaig) adds the next two, convincing the father that his son has forced her. Ronan has his son killed, and his fosterson (Congal) and the jester who try to defend their fellow are also killed. The surviving fosterbrothers avenge them by cutting off the heads of Eochaid and his sons and flinging them at Eochaid's daughter. That brutal vengeance on her family causes her to commit suicide; she does not, like Phaedra, kill herself to make the king believe her. Some characters are mentioned in the Annals (see no. 96 below), but the story is fiction.

## [ 70 ]
# Ronan with His Dead Son
*Is úar fri clói ngaíthe*

EOCHAID S DAUGHTER

1. It is cold against the whirlwind
   for anyone who herds Aife's cattle.

1. Cold in the whirlwind girding
   for Aife's cattle herding.

MAEL FOTHARTAIG

It is a vain herding
without cows, without anyone who loves.

Vain herding: no cows coming
nor anyone for loving.

RONAN

2. It is a cold wind
   at the door of the warrior's house;
   dear were the warriors
   that were between me and the wind.

2. Cold the wind
   past the warrior's house skimmed;
   dear the warriors I would find
   between me and winds that whined.

3. Sleep, daughter of Eochaid,
   the bitterness of the wind is great
   sorrow to me Mael Fothartaig
   killed for the sin of a wanton woman.

3. Sleep now, daughter of Eochaid,
   bitterly winds are stinging;
   woe is me, Mael Fothartaig
   slain for a woman's sinning.

4. Sleep, daughter of Eochaid;
   I do not sleep until you sleep,
   seeing Mael Fothartaig
   in his shirt full of blood.

4. Sleep now, daughter of Eochaid,
   I rest not till thou'rt sleeping,
   looking on Mael Fothartaig
   in his shirt of blood steeping.

EOCHAID'S DAUGHTER

5. Alas, dead one in the corner,
   that all eyes pass by,
   what we did of sin
   was your pain after rejecting you.

5. Woe is me, corpse laid yonder
   toward whom all eyes would wander;
   what we committed of sin
   was thy pain, since rejecting.

RONAN

6. Sleep, daughter of Eochaid,
   the men are not crazy;
   though you have wet your cloak,
   that is not my son whom you keen.

6. Sleep now, daughter of Eochaid,
   mad men might take thy scheming,
   though thy damp cloak thou smearest,
   not my dearest thou'rt keening.

Meter: st 1, 7₂ throughout, *deibide* with rhythmic rime; st 2, 3₁7₁7₁7₁, *deibide* with rhythmic rime; stt 3–4, 7₂7₂7₂7₂, rime 2/4; st 5, *deibide* with rhythmic rime 1/2; st 6, 7₂ throughout, rime 2/4, linking rime 3/4. Rimes are sometimes imperfect.

{ 71 }

# After Vengeance Ronan and the Hounds Lament His Son
## Ro-gab Eochaid oenléni

1. Eochaid took a single shirt
   after being in a long, warm cloak;
   the grief that is on Dun Naas,
   it is on Dun Severick.

2. Give food, give drink
   to Mael Fothartaig's hound,
   and let someone else give
   food to Congal's hound.

3. Give food, give drink
   to Mael Fothartaig's hound,
   the hound of a man who would give food
   to anyone, whatever price he had to pay.

4. A grief to me, the beating of Dathlenn
   with rods of metal across her sides;
   it is not our reproach to her,
   it was not she who sold our fair ones.

5. Doilin
   to me whom you served;
   her head in each lap in turn
   seeking someone she will not find.

[Alternate, after a suggestion of Greene's]

6. The men, the youths, the horses
   used to be about Mael Fothartaig;
   they were not envious of anyone's
       protection
   while their leader was alive.

7. The men, the youths, the horses
   used to be about Mael Fothartaig;

---

1. Eochaid has one covering
   since his cape of leveret;
   the sorrow filling Dun Naas
   the same is on Dun Severick.

2. Give food and give drink from me
   to hound of Mael Fothartaig,
   but someone else preferring
   to Congal's hound offering.

3. Give food and give drink from me
   to hound of Mael Fothartaig—
   hound of one open-handed
   whatever price demanded.

4. Alas, Dathlenn quivering,
   rods beat her sides the sharper;
   no blame is she incurring:
   my dears she did not barter.

5. Doilini
   has served me appealingly,
   her head on each lap by turns
   she yearns for one feelingly.

5. Doilini
   has served me appealingly,
   her head on each lap she whined
   seeking one she cannot find.

6. The men, youths, horses—all three
   were about Mael Fothartaig;
   no care for defense while he,
   their leader, lived happily.

7. The men, youths, horses—all three
   were about Mael Fothartaig;

they used to be out without restraint;
they would run horse races.

out on the plain without check
horses racing breakneck.

8. The men, the youths, the horses
used to be about Mael Fothartaig;
there were at frequent times
shouts after permanent victories.

8. The men, youths, horses—all three
were about Mael Fothartaig;
often they cried the story
after lasting victory.

9. The household of Mael Fothartaig,
I agree they were not dishonored;
not well they stood by the man
who would come in need.

9. The house of Mael Fothartaig—
honor I conceded 'em;
not well they stood by a man
who came when they needed 'im.

10. My son, Mael Fothartaig,
to whom the long woods were a
dwelling;
kings nor princes did not unyoke
without keeping watch for him.

10. My own son, Mael Fothartaig,
for whom tall trees were dwelling,
neither kings nor royalty
unyoked, no watch compelling.

11. My son, Mael Fothartaig,
rode around Scotland of coasts;
he was a hero among heroes;
he used to impose his rule on them.

11. My own son, Mael Fothartaig,
rides 'round Scotland of gorses,
warrior of war companies,
on them his rule he forces.

12. My son, Mael Fothartaig,
he as a champion of the hound pack,
a tall white salmon flashing;
he has taken a cold dwelling.

12. My own son, Mael Fothartaig,
hero of houndpacks boldest,
long lithe champion flashing
takes a dwelling—the coldest.

Meter: stt 1 and 9, $7_37_37_17_3$, rime 2/4; stt 2, 6–8, *deibide* (st 6, rhythmic rime 1/3); st 3, *deibide* with rhythmic rime 3/4; stt 4 and 12, $7_37_27_27_2$, rime 2/4; st 5, $3_37_37_17_3$, rime 1/2/4 (not perfect); alt st 5, *deibide* with short first line and rhythmic rime; stt 10–11, $7_37_27_37_2$, rime 2/4.

# [ 72–90 ]
## FROM THE FINN CYCLE

# [ 72–74 ]
# Of Diarmait and Grainne

One of the most durable stories from the Finn Cycle is that of Diarmait's elopement with Grainne, the wife or promised bride of Finn mac Cumail. Since Diarmait was one of Finn's most important followers, his loyalty is divided. But Grainne forces herself upon him, after drugging her father, Finn, and most of the fian (Finn's warrior-band) at her betrothal banquet.

The lullaby (no. 74) is in the form of a dialogue: Grainne sings and Diarmait replies.

## [ 72 ]
# Grainne in Love with Diarmait
### *Fil duine*

There is someone
whom I would thank at sight (of him);
to whom I would give the fertile earth,
all, all though it were a poor bargain.

That fellow,
  I give thanks, him regarding;
for him I'd sell earth—yellow,
  mellow, all—though bad bargain.

Meter: $3_27_27_27_2$; rime 1/3, 2/4; linking rime 3/4.

## [ 73 ]
# Grainne's Forest Fare †
### *Is maith do chuit, a Gráinne*

Grainne, your meat is good,
it is better for you than a kingdom:
the delicacy of woodcocks
with a drop of fine mead.

Grainne, your meal good faring
better weal than king's dining:
  besides choice woodcocks ready,
drops of heady mead shining.

Meter: $7_2$ throughout; rime 2/4 with final syllables of 1/2/3 riming; internal rime 1/2; linking rime 3/4.

## [ 74 ]
# Sleepsong of Grainne
### *Cotail becán becán bec*

1. Sleep a little, a little bit,
  for no little thing is to be feared by you,
  boy to whom I have given love,
  Diarmait, son of O'Duibne.

2. Sleep here soundly, soundly,
  descendant of Duibne, excellent
    Diarmait;
  I shall keep watch for you,
  comely son of O'Duibne.

3. Sleep a little (a blessing on you)
  above the water of Trengort Well,

1. Sleep a little, a little bit;
  for you no fear, not a bit,
    lad for whom I loved and lived,
    son of O'Duibne, Diarmait.

2. Sleep here soundly, deep and long,
  Duibne's grandson, Diarmait strong,
    safely a while, watched by me,
    O'Duibne's son, the shapely.

3. Sleep a little (blessings yours)
  above Trengort Well waters,

lake surface of foam
from the edge of the Land of Strong
      Streams.

4. May it be the same as the sleep of the
         south
   of good Fidach of the chief poets,
   when he took the daughter of long-
         lived Morann
   in spite of Conall from the Redbranch.

5. May it be the same as the sleep of the
         north
   of fair handsome Finnchad of Assaroe,
   when he took Slaine (happy lot)
   in spite of hard-headed Failbe.

6. May it be the same as the sleep of the
         west
   of Aine, daughter of Gailian,
   when once she went a journey, hair in
         tresses,*
   with Dubthach from Dairinis (Isle of
         oaks).

7. May it be the same as the sleep of the
         east
   of gifted, daring Dedad,
   when he took Coinchenn, daughter of
         Benn,
   in spite of staunch Deichell of the dark
         point.

8. Valiant defense of western Greece,
   I shall stay keeping watch for you;
   my heart will all but break
   if I fail for a moment seeing you.

9. Parting the two of us
   is parting the children of one dwelling,
   it is parting body from soul,
   warrior of the Lake of lovely Carman.

10. An incantation will be consigned to
         your track
    (Caeilte's course will not be improper),

*Flowing hair is often a sign of an unmarried girl.

light foam on lakes at land's edge
of stilled strong streams once savage.

4. Sleep as in the south afar
   good Fidach, the high scholar,
      who took Morann's girl to bed
      despite Conall of Branch-red.

5. Sleep as in the north below
   Finnchad Fair of Assaroe,
      who snatched Slaine, lucky win,
      despite Failbe Chotachinn.

6. Sleep as in the west away
   daughter of Gailian, Aine,
      who went, hair hanging, soft smile,
      with Dubthach come from Oak-isle.

7. Sleep as in the east, O lad,
   as doughty, daring Dedad,
      who stole Benn's Coinchenn apart
      despite Deichell of Dark-dart.

8. I shall remain with you to guard,
   great champion of Greece westward;
      my heart will break, not endure,
      if sight of you meets failure.

9. Parting us two among men
   is parting fellow children,
      or body from soul undone,
      O warrior of Loch Carman.

10. Caeilte's course brings no foul play;
    charms we'll lay on your pathway;

that death nor grief may come to you,
and you may not be left in eternal
    sleep.

no grief nor death on you fall,
leave you in sleep eternal.

DIARMAIT:

11. The stag in the east does not sleep;
he does not stop bellowing;
    though he is among the oaks of the
      blackbirds,
there is no thought of sleep.

11. No sleep: the stag of the east
bellows not less but increased,
    though among oaks blackbirds cling
    their thoughts are not on sleeping.

12. The hornless doe does not sleep,
calling for her speckled fawn;
    she takes a course across the tops of
      bushes;
she does not sleep in her lair.

12. No sleep: the bare-headed hind
cries for her fawn with flecked-side;
    she flies past tips that swing,
    lies not in her lair sleeping.

13. The lively linnet does not sleep
above the tops of the beautiful tangled
      trees;
they are loud-voiced there;
though the thrush does not sleep.

13. No sleep: the swift singer flees
o'er tangled tops of tall trees
    with loud music—hear him sing—
    nor is proud thrush yet sleeping.

14. The perfect duck does not sleep:
her vigor in skilled swimming is good;
she does not slumber nor rest there;
she does not sleep in her nest.

14. No sleep for the dainty duck,
swimming through reed and tussock;
    sleep and slumber do not bring
    to her nest any sleeping.

15. Tonight the curlew does not sleep;
above the fury of the very high tempest;
the sound of his clear voice is sweet;
among streams it does not sleep.

15. The curlew does not sleep tonight
above the raging storm's height;
    their crying, quiv'ring calls ring,
    among sheer streams no sleeping.
    Sleep.

Meter: *deibide* with rhythmic rimes in stt 1, 2, and 5; internal rime in 3/4 of st 4, 5, 12, 13, and 15; abundant alliteration.

{ 75–79 }

# The Conversation of the Old Men

The *Accallam na Senórach* is an account of the return of Oisin son of Finn and Caeilte, another Fenian warrior from the Otherworld. They meet St. Patrick and talk to him of past glory when Finn was leader of the fianna. The saint records their stories, now and then worrying about their paganism, but too fascinated to abandon listening or recording.

## { 75 }
## Caeilte Speaks of Finn †
### *Dámad ór in duille donn*

If the brown leaf were gold
that the woods shed,
if the bright wave were silver
Finn would have given (them) away.

If lost leaves were gold so bright
that forests let fall,
if wan waves were silver white,
Finn would have giv'n all.

Meter: 7,5,7,5,; rime 1/3, 2/4.

## { 76 }
## Arran †
### *Arann na n-aiged n-imda*

1. Arran of the many stags,
   the sea coming against its shoulder,
   an island in which troops are fed,
   a ridge on which the blue spear is
   reddened.

2. Foolish deer on its peaks,
   sweet bogberries on its bushes,
   cold water in its rivers,
   acorns on the brown oaktrees.

3. Greyhounds on it and beagles,
   blackberries and dark sloes of the
   blackthorn,
   its seawall close to the trees,
   deer scattering among the oaks.

4. Gleaning of purple on its rocks,
   flawless grass on her hillslopes,
   above her rocks, beauty of ornament,
   gamboling of speckled fawns a-leaping.

5. Smooth her plain, fat her swine,
   pleasant her fields, a tale that is to be
   believed,
   nuts on the tip of her hazelwood,
   sailing of longships past her.

6. Beautiful for them when good weather
   comes,
   trout under the banks of its rivers,

1. Arran with deer droves running,
   the barren breakers pounding,
   where troops eat on that island—
   highland with blades abounding.

2. Its deer merry on mountains,
   each berry bright in bracken,
   cold currents in the reaches,
   brown beeches their nuts fatten.

3. Greyhounds and beagles hunting;
   sloes and blackberries dark'ning;
   its cliffs close to the holtwood;
   oakwood where stags stray hark'ning.

4. Her crags, crimson crops growing;
   graceful grasses are swaying;
   above her rocks enchanting
   panting freckled fawns playing.

5. Fine her fields, fat her farrows,
   fair her folds—happy hiding—
   nuts the hazel is bearing;
   far-faring ships go gliding.

6. Fair times no doubt are finest;
   trout in streams, no stretch barren,

seagulls answer around her white cliffs,      round the scarp seagulls screaming
fair each season of Arran.               each dreaming hour in Arran. Arran.

Meter: 7₂ throughout; rime 2/4; stt 1, 2, and 6, internal rime 1/2; stt 3 and 4, consonance between final words 1/2/4; st 5, internal assonance 1/2 (I have substituted internal consonance in the imitative translation). Nineteen of the twenty-four lines have alliteration.

# [ 77 ]
# Well of the Strand of Two Women †
*A thopair Trága Dá Ban*

1. Well of the Shore of Two Women,
   beautiful your bright-tipped cress
   since your crop has been forsaken by you,
   growth is not permitted to your
       brooklime.

2. Your trout out from your riverbanks,
   your wild pigs in your desert,
   stags of your rocks, fair hunting,
   your speckled red-breasted fawns.

3. Your acorns from the tips of your trees,
   your fish in the mouths of your rivers:
   beautiful the color of your sprigs of
       arum,
   on green foliage of the forests.

4. It is from you the fianna went
   when Coinchenn, equally generous, was
       killed,
   when Finn's fian was slaughtered
   in the morning above Maelglenn.

5. From you went Fathad of feasts,
   he was a hero who suffered anxiety,
   when he received a gift in eastern lands,
   when he died in the battle of Clarach.

6. Above the well came Blai,
   daughter of Derg Dianscothach (Red
       Very Eloquent),
   she wept aloud in her lamentation
   as the battle of Confait was fought.

1. O Well of Two Women's Strand,
   fair your cress topping clean-sand,
       since deserted is your crop,
       your brooklime can't develop.

2. Your streaked trout from the stream's
       bank,
   your tawny fawns with flecked-flank,
       stags for hunting mid rocks lurk,
       wild swine here in your desert.

3. Acorns from the oaktree's tip,
   your fish beneath the ledge-lip,
       colored sprigs of lilies lure,
       pale green, reflecting verdure.

4. From you went the roving bands
   when fell Coinchenn of freehands,
       when death fell on fians of Finn
       above Maelglenn that morning.

5. From you went Fathad of Feast,
   hero who found in far-east
       both gifts and grief in full
       dying in Clarach's battle.

6. Beyond the well she did not stir,
   Blai, Derg Dianscothaig's daughter;
       wailing she wept against fate
       when they fought the fight Confait.

7. After the dying of hound and men,
   after the wounding of very bright heroes,
   she heard the clear call of Garad
   at night beside the well.

7. After death of hounds and men,
   after maiming great guardsmen,
   she heard a call—Garad's yell—
   at night beside the wan-well. Well.

Meter: *deibide* with much alliteration.

# [ 78 ]
# The Sons of Lugaid †
*Trí tuile*

1. Three floods
   that used to come from the high fort of
   Ruide:
   a flood of warriors, a flood of horses,
   a flood of greyhounds of the sons of
   Lugaid.

1. Thrice flooding
   from Ruide's high fort running:
   flood of horses, flood of men,
   flood of hounds, Lugaid's huntsmen.

2. Three kinds of music
   for goodly successful kings:
   harp music, music of timpans* famous,
   the humming of Fer Tuinne, son of
   Trogan.

2. Three musics
   for the lucky kings coming:
   harp tones, timbrel tones that sing
   Fer Tuinne tuneful humming.

3. Three noises
   that are without pause:
   the sound of sheep on the meadow,
   the sound of horse-racing, and the
   sound of cattle.

3. Three noises
   unceasing, never slowing:
   bleating sheep on green grazing,
   horse-racing, cattle lowing.

4. Three noises:
   the sound of swine, hump-backed,
   excellent,
   the sound of an army on the lawn of the
   hostel,
   sound of merriment and sound of mead.

4. Three clamors:
   grunting hogs, hump-backed,
   splendid,
   warcries before fort fronting,
   drunken mirth when mead's ended.

5. Three crops
   that are there above the branches:
   a crop falling, a frequent course,
   a crop in bloom and a crop ripe.

5. Three products
   were high on branches looming:
   a crop falling, as it might,
   crop that's ripe, a crop blooming.

6. Lugaid abandoned three sons
   where had their work gone?

6. Lugaid left three sons, raiders,
   where went their labors, family?

*A stringed instrument.

Ruide son of Lugaid, the stout one,
Echaid and Fiacha the manly.

Echaid and Ruide portly,
    courtly Fiacha, the manly.

7. I give witness of Echaid
   who did not go a step in retreat;
   he did not utter a word too much,
   nor was anyone greater or braver.

7. Echaid's praise I'm declaring,
       faring no step defeated;
   no words did he speak in vain,
       his fame: none braver greeted.

8. I give witness of Fiacha:
   where has his plunder gone?
   He was not without accustomed
       minstrelsy;
   there was not a time without drinking
       beer.

8. Fiacha's praise I am telling,
       his plunder gone aglinting;
   not without accustomed song,
       not long without beer drinking.

9. I give witness of Ruide,
   to whom used to come the three floods:
   Ruide never denied anyone anything
   and he sought nothing from anyone.

9. Ruide's praise I am speaking:
       three floods around him sweeping;
   Ruide refused none who sought,
       asked naught from other's keeping.

10. Thirty princes, thirty chieftains,
    thirty champions, a course for a king,
    this was the number of his hundredfold
        troop
    thirty hundred times three.

10. Thirty princes, thirty chiefs,
        thirty heroes, roll precise;
    hundredfold troops in number,
        thirty hundred once, twice, thrice.
    Thrice.

Meter: st 1, *deibide*; stt 2 and 5, $3_27_27_17_2$; stt 3 and 4, $3_27_27_27_2$; st 6, $7_2$ through-
out; stt 7–9, $7_27_27_17_2$; st 10, $7_17_17_27_1$; st 1, rhythmic rime 1/2, rime 3/4; stt
2–10, rime 2/4; st 9, rime 1/2/4; stt 3–10, linking rime 3/4; stt 6–7, linking
rime 1/2.

# [ 79 ]
# Creide's Lament for Cael
### *Géisid cúan*

1. The bay roars,
   above the red surge of Rinn Da Barc;
   the drowning of the warrior of Loch Da
       Chonn,
   it is that the wave along the shore
       keens.

1. Cries the cove:
       moan of fierce flood Rinn Da Barc;
   the man from Loch Da Chonn drowned,
       keened by sound of wave on rock.

2. Let the heron call
   in the marsh of the Ridge of Da Thren:
   she does not protect her living ones:
   a fox of two colors is on the track of her
       birds.

2. Calls the crane
       at bog Druim Da Thren she wails;
   no help for young who'd elude
       the two-hued fox on their trails.

3. Sad the cry
   that the thrush makes on Druim Cain;
   and not less sad the call
   that the blackbird makes in Leitir Laig.

4. Sad the sound
   the stag makes in Druim Da Leis:
   a hind is dead on Druim Silenn;
   the great stag roars after her.

5. To me a hardship
   is the death of the warrior who used to
      lie with me:
   that the son of the woman from Daire
      Da Dos
   should be with a cross above his head.

6. I find a hardship Cael
   being in the state of death by my side,
   a wave coming across his bright side:
   it is that has bewildered me, the extent
      of his beauty.

7. Sad the call
   that the wave of the shore makes on the
      strand:
   since it has drowned a noble handsome
      man,
   it is a hardship to me that Cael went to
      meet it.

8. Sad the noise
   that the wave makes on the northern
      shore,
   dashing about the handsome rock,
   keening for Cael since he passed away.

9. Sad the struggle
   that the wave makes on the southern
      shore;
   as for me, my lifetime has passed:
   the worse my appearance, as is known.

10. Strange melody
    that the heavy wave makes at Tulach Leis;
    as for me, my treasure is no more
    since it boasted of the news it roared to
       me.

3. Sad the keen
   of thrushes upon Druim Chain;
      blackbirds, not less sad their song
   along Leitir Laig unseen.

4. Sad the call,
   on Druimlesh the stag stands tall;
      on Druim Silenn, dead the doe;
   in woe the strong stag will bawl.

5. Grief to me
   his death who once lay with me;
      son of one in Derry Dos,
   a cross above him I see.

6. For Cael, grief:
   beside me dead—no relief;
      the wave went o'er his white side,
   he died: beauty past belief.

7. Sad the sound
   when waves along the strand pound;
      my grief that Cael wandered there,
   since that fair fine man has drowned.

8. Sad the roar
   Waves make on the northern shore,
      tumult round a rugged rock
   in shock that Cael is no more.

9. Sad the strife
   waves make on the southern hithe.
      My time has come, all know now
   my brow tholed the worst of life.

10. Music strange,
    at Tulach Leis waves rage high;
       gone my dear—no more to lose—
    news, a bitter boast, they cry.

11. Dead is the swan,
    mournful her mate after her;
    much feeling it gives me,
    the sorrow that affects the swan.

12. Since the son of Crimthan drowned,
    there is none dear to me after him;
    many a chieftain fell by his hand;
    his shield in a day of danger did not
        roar.

11. Dead the swan,
    gloomy her mate and she gone;
      great feeling to me was taught
    by sorrow that caught the swan.

12. Since the son of Crimthann drowned
    I found none dear—none have I.
    By his hand great chieftains fell;
    his shield gave no yell, no cry. Cries.

Meter: 3₁7₁7₁7₁ except st 12, 7₂7₁7₁7₁; stt 1, 10, and 12 linking rime 1/2; stt 1–2, 10, and 12, rime 2/4; stt 3–9 and 11, rime 1/2/4. Only st 2 lacks any rime link in 1/2.

## [ 80—90 ]
# From the Songbook of Finn

The rest of the poems of the Finn Cycle given here nave no prose frame. Indeed, Grainne's Sleepsong is one of these, but it belongs to a story we do have in prose. These others come from a part of the cycle that we know only from these poems. They are not narrative ballads like "Sir Patrick Spens" or the Robin Hood ballads, but more like "Edward, Edward" or "Lord Randall" as a speech or occasionally a dialogue between the Fenian heroes. St. Patrick, too, sometimes joins in, but mostly Caeilte (a member of the fian) or Oisin (Finn's son) is talking in praise of the great hounds, great horses, and great men of the past contrasted with the puny creatures of a later day. The scorn of the bells and preaching echoes poems from the Suibne story and is hinted at in poem no. 2 on the blackbird. Oisin's regret for his youth is a familiar theme, not so very different from the complaint of the Old Woman of Beare (no. 46), though less confident of salvation.

## [ 80 ]
# Beagles Bay on the Hill of Kings †
### Guth gadair i cCnoc na Ríg

1. The voice of a beagle on the hill of
      kings:
    dear to me the mound where it is;
    often we had a fian's fireplace
    between the mountain and the sea.

2. Here were the followers of Finn,
    young men to whom the sound of
      strings was sweet;

1. Bay of beagle, hill of kings,
    dear it rings, and dear the *sid*;
    we often built the fian's fire
    no higher than 'twixt crag and sea.

2. Here were followers of Finn
    who found a string gave sweet notes;

dear to me the wild band
who went on journeys of many
    hundreds.

3. It seemed to us their hunt was
    splendid;
many red stags fell by their prowess;
many swift spotted hounds
coming to meet them on the mountain.

4. Bran and Sceolang the beautiful,
his own hounds in the hands of the
    king;
those hounds were dear to Finn;
good were their mettle and their deeds.

5. Cnu Deireoil in the king's breast,
good son of Lug of fair form,
he would play the harp for Finn,
the fair-haired man with a great voice.

6. Each chief of nine of the fian
used to come himself to the king
to hold great hunts
that the company made on Druim
    Cain.

7. Fifty stags of many points
fell by my own hand, O king,
likewise fifty boars,
although tonight I am without
    anything.

8. The children of Ronan the red had a
    camp
on the northern side of the glen;
splendid was the Fenians' fire
that the fian made at the foot of the
    mountain.

9. Clan Morna was a wild band
with many of man on the southern side,
often they would fight a hard battle
and would come victorious out of it.

10. I heard a red beagle's voice
on the slope beside the stream;

---

dear the wild band that rode forth,
    many hundreds with high hopes.

3. Splendid hunters they appear:
    the red deer fell through their skill;
many a swift spotted hound
    coming toward them 'round the hill.

4. Bran and Sceolang, fairest known,
    his own hounds, leashed by the king;
good for courage, good for deed,
    dear in need those hounds of Finn.

5. Cnu Deireol at the king's breast,
    best son of Lug of fine form,
for Finn the harp he would play,
    that fey fellow of loud song.

6. The fian's chiefs of nine would come
    to run great hunts on the hill;
circling Druim Cain the host spread
    by Finn led with hunting skill.

7. Fifty stags, all antlered well,
    by my hand fell in king's sight;
besides these fifty wild swine,
    though nothing is mine tonight.

8. Sons of Ronan Ruad set forth
    from camp on north in the glen;
splendidly the full fian fared
    on food prepared by her men.

9. Sons of Morna, crazy troop,
    many group on southern side;
often they fought a hard fray
    and came away with due pride.

10. I've heard red beagles' voices fill
    the hill toward streams that fall,
    play;

it raised wrinkles on my head,
the cry of the beagle is a sweet sound.

at the sound my heart leaps high,
the beagle's cry, a sweet-voiced bay.
Bay.

11. I am Oisin, son of the king,
it is long since my shape withered;
although my heart is sick,
nevertheless the sound is musical to us.

11. I am Oisin, son of king,
withered skin, long gone this day;
though heart is sore, body weak,
I find sweet the beagle's bay. Bay.

Meter: 7₁ throughout; rime 2/4; stt 1 and 3–11, rime 1/2, 3/4; st 2, linking rime 1/2 only; alliteration frequent.

## [ 81 ]
# A Bell Rings on the Red Ridge †
*Faíd cluic do-chúala i nDruim Deirg*

OISIN

1. "The ringing of a bell I have heard on
Red Ridge
where the fian used to hunt;
I never heard before that
the sound of a bell in a hunting forest."

1. "A bell heard on Red Ridge front
where the full fian used to hunt;
I never before heard ring
a bell in wood for hunting."

PATRICK

2. "The ringing of a bell I have heard on
Red Ridge
where the fian used to hunt;
and I have not heard before
a single sound that was sweeter."

2. "A bell heard on Red Ridge front
where the full fian used to hunt;
I never heard, I aver,
one sound that was sweeter."

OISIN

3. "The ringing of a bell I have heard on
Red Ridge
where the fian used to hunt;
sweeter to me at the coming of the
army
was the roar of the Fian gathering
there.

3. "A bell heard on Red Ridge front
where the full fian used to hunt;
sweeter to me the band comes
as the fian's call then summons.

4. "The ringing of a bell I have heard on
Red Ridge
where the fian used to hunt;
sweeter to me on going out
was the whistle the son of Lugach used
to give.

4. "A bell I heard on Red Ridge front
where the full fian used to hunt;
sweeter taking to the path
at whistle of Mac Lugach.

5. "Seldom by the wood of Red Ridge
   was the ringing of a bell from slope to
      slope;
   more often for the litter of wolves
   has the late night been bitter cold.

6. "Who is this miserable cleric to the west
   who strikes his little bell fiercely,
   who does not listen to the voice of the
      hounds
   that is in the glen near him?"

PATRICK

7. "Though the voice of the hounds seems
      sweet to you
   and though it be a cause of high spirits,
   sweeter to the King is one
   who listens to the cleric's sermon."

OISIN

8. "Though you think sweet what they say
   and though your mind think it good,
   the roar of the maddened stag is sweeter
   than the music the clerics sing.

9. "I have seen men on the plain
   who would not listen to the voice of the
      bell,
   and who would leave dead together
   you and all your clerics.

10. "Sweeter to me at the time of rising
    heathcocks on mountain peaks
    than the voice of the cleric inside
    bleating and baaing."

PATRICK

11. "Oisin, tell the news
    and leave us not in disgrace:
    what would they do to me for it,
    for striking this little bell?"

OISIN

12. "I truly give my word,
    I swear by my king's soul,
    he would beat your bell on your head
    until you were without life.

5. "Seldom on Red Ridge remote
   a bell rang from slope to slope;
   often late night chill stirring
   left the wolf-pack shivering.

6. "Who's this cleric so absurd
   who beats so hard the bell heard?
   nor hears he the howl of hound
   near him in the glen, gladsound."

7. "Though howl of hound give you glee
   and spirits rise, heart happy,
   he is dearer to the King
   who to cleric is list'ning."

8. "Though sweet to you what they say
   and good to thought as guideway,
   sweeter the roar of stag swift
   than music sung by cleric.

9. "I have seen men on the fell
   who would not hark to your bell,
   but would leave all of you dead,
   you and your clerics vaunted.

10. "At rising sweeter to me
    heathcocks on mountain peaks free
    than a cleric's voice within
    like a sheep or goat bleating."

11. "Oisin, tell it to my face
    and leave us not in disgrace:
    what would they do to me then
    for striking this bell often?"

12. "Truly I give my word there
    and by my king's soul I swear,
    he'd beat the bell on your head
    until your soul departed.

13. "If fierce Garb Doire heard
the noise of the bell in this church in
the west,
he would quickly go inside
and would break the cleric's bell.

14. "If Finn the warrior heard
the noise of your little bell, cleric,
he would have gone to meet you
and you would not get out of it.

15. "If Conan of the fian heard
the noise of this bell [coming] toward
me from the west,
though all the clerics of the world were
there,
they would all be without life.

16. "If dear Caeilte heard,
a man who did not refuse combat,
he would have gone in, no lie,
and have broken your little bells.

17. "Alas, it is torment to my heart
separating from the slope of Maenmag,
and from those honorable champions,
from my fian and from my good poets.

18. "I am Oisin, good son of Finn,
I believe in God above, Adzehead
(Patrick),
though tonight I am without fian,
without treasure,
a pain for me is the noise of the little
bell."

13. "If rough Doire dread should hear
this bell ring in this cell near,
he would quickly go inside
and shatter the bell broadside.

14. "If it were the warrior Finn
who heard your little bell ring,
he'd have pursued you no doubt,
nor could you make a breakout.

15. "Had Conan the Fenian heard
the sound of this bell disturb,
though all earth's clerics were there,
all would die from his warfare.

16. "If it were Caeilte heard that,
one who refused no combat,
he would have come rushing in
and ended your bell's ringing.

17. "Alas, the hurt to my heart
from slopes of Maenmag to part
from my fian, poets who sung,
and all those heroes handsome.

18. "I am Oisin, Finn's good son,
great God above, my loved one,
tonight no fian, no wealth found,
yet pain to me the bell-sound. Bell."

Meter: *deibide* with rhythmic rime 1/2 in stt 1–6 and 9–15.

# [ 82 ]
# The Death of Finn's Hound Conbecc †
### *Trúag lem aided Chonbicce*

1. Painful to me was Conbecc's violent
death;
Conbecc, his smoothness was great;
I have not seen one more nimble-footed
after wild swine or deer.

1. Grievous Conbecc's grim slaughter—
Conbecc—great was his sleekness;
I've seen no more trim stalker
of swine or deer for fleetness.

2. A hurt to me was Conbecc's violent
       death,
   Conbecc of the rough voice;
   I have not seen one more nimble-footed
   killing a stag without hesitation.

2. Painful Conbecc's grim slaughter—
       Conbecc of hollow howling—
   I've seen no more trim stalker
       quick-killing stags and growling.

3. A hurt to me was Conbecc's violent
       death,
   above the high green waves;
   his violent death was cause of strife;
   his death, great was its sorrow.

3. Painful Conbecc's grim slaughter
       on great green billows heaving;
   his end brought war's slim quarter;
       his death, great was its grieving.
       Grievous.

Meter: $7_37_27_37_2$; rime 2/4; consonance 1/3.

## [ 83 ]
## Caeilte Sang of Strength Departed †
### *Bec in-nocht lúth mo dá lúa*

1. Tonight the energy of my two heels is
       small,
   I know my body is flesh:
   the running of my feet was good
   until Patrick (the Adzehead) came.

1. Little tonight my foot's force,
       my form is mere flesh, of course;
       lithe my legs, speeding ahead,
       until arrived the Adzehead.

2. My two feet were swift,
   my eyes kept watch in my head,
   my hands fed the scaldcrows,
   my weapons were not without a shout
       of victory.

2. Swift on foot toward each border;
       in my head eyes for warder;
       my hands would feed hooded crows;
       my blows brought cheers and order.

3. I used to go on horses,
   over any great champion I had the
       upper hand;
   I used to guard the honor of Finn,
   I was fierce, fierce in difficulties.

3. I used to ride on horses;
   I conquered champion forces,
       guarded the honor of Finn,
   I was grim in tight courses.

4. I and Oisin son of Finn,
   our blows we struck together;*
   our deeds were great,
   our boasts were small.

4. I and Oisin, son of Finn,
       our beating blows were mickle;
   our grand deeds were not lagging,
   yet was our bragging little. Little.

Meter: st 1, *deibide*, rhythmic rimes 1/2; stt 2 and 3, $7_27_27_17_2$, rime 1/2/4, link-
ing rime 3/4; st 4, $7_17_27_27_2$, rime 2/4, linking rime 3/4.

*Meyer: "in unison."

{ 84 }

# Caeilte Returns to the Mound of the Fian

*Forud na Fíann fás in-nocht*

1. Empty tonight is the Mound of the Fian
   to which Finn of the bare edge used to
        come;
   at the death of that prince without sorrow
   great, noble Allen is empty.

2. The good retinue does not live;
   Finn the true prince does not live;
   the band unconcealed is not
   around the king nor leader.

3. All Finn's warrior-band is dead
   though they once went from glen to glen;
   ill I am after the splendid kings,
   after Diarmait and Conan,

4. After Goll Mac Morna of the plain
   and Ailill of hundreds,
   after the end of Eogan of the gray lance
   and of Conall of the first attack.

5. I tell you beforehand;
   it is true what I say:
   our loss there is great
   without black Drumann of spear-hurling.

6. After the destruction of the bands and
        the hundreds,
   it is sad that I did not find death there,
   after their going from border to border
   though once crowded was the mound.

1. Forad na Fian waste is laid
   where once came brave Finn bare-blade;
       since death of that fearless Finn,
       waste lies his great Allen.

2. Finn, fine chief, no more on mold;
   no more his hearty household;
       no more captain and bold band
       surround fian's lord and moorland.

3. Dead are all Finn's Fenian men,
   though once they roved glen to glen;
       ill-luck mine with choice chiefs gone,
       after Diarmait and Conan.

4. Since Goll mac Morn' of the Moor,
   Ailill of hundred splendor,
       since loss of Eogan dark-dart
       and Conall, first on rampart.

5. I tell you further this thing—
   it is true what I'm saying—
       great our lack without that one,
       straight dart-driving Dub Drumann.

6. Since these hosts and hundreds fell,
   alas I died not as well;
       end to end the way they trod:
       once packed, now waste lies Forad.
       Forad.

Meter: *deibide* with rhythmic rimes 1/2 in stt 3 and 6.

{ 85 }

# Music of the World †

*Binn guth duine i dTír in Óir*

1. Man's voice in the Land of Gold is
        musical,
   musical the language that birds chant;

1. Sweet, man's voice in Land of Gold;
       sweet and bold birdsongs resound;

musical is the cry the crane makes,
musical is the wave in Bun Da Threoir.

sweet call of cranes, waves long roar
   on shore Bun Da Threoir—sweet
      sound.

2. The sound that the wind makes is
     musical,
  the voice of the cuckoo above Caise Con
    is musical;
  the splendor that the sun makes is
    beautiful,
  from the west the whistling of the
    blackbird is musical.

2. Sweet the wind's whine, sweet the cry
    cuckoos high o'er Caise Con,
  fair the shining sun by day,
    sweet and gay the blackbird's song.

3. The voice of the eagle of Assaroe is
     musical
  above the harbor of great Morna's son;
  the cuckoo's voice above the tops of the
    thicket is musical;
  the pause that the crane makes is
    beautiful.

3. Sweet at Assaroe the scream
    of earn seen at Mac Morn's Bay;
  sweet cuckoo's note above brush,
    fair hush as cranecalls stay.

4. Finn, son of Cumall, my own father,
  in his warrior band were seven keen
    battalions;
  when we let the hounds at the deer,
  musical was their cry on its track.

4. For Finn mac Cool, father mine,
    sev'n prime corps his fian complete;
  hounds unleashed to deer as prey,
    their hunting bay ever sweet. Sweet.

Meter: 7₁ throughout; rime 2/4; st 1, end consonance 1/2/4, linking rime 3/4; st 2, end consonance 2/3/4, linking rime 3/4; st 3, linking rime 1/2, line 4 consonance and rime imperfect 1/2/4; st 4, linking rime 1/2, consonance 1/3.

## [ 86 ]
## A Dreary Night in Elphin †
*Is fada anocht i n-Oil Finn*

1. It is long tonight in Oil Finn (Elphin);
  it seemed long to us last night,
  though today was long for me,
  yesterday was long enough.

1. Weary tonight in Oil Finn,
    weary within last night too;
  today was weary though gone;
    yesterday as long, 'tis true.

2. Every day that comes seems long to me;
  not like that was customary for us;
  my being absent from the Fenians
  has put my mind backwards.

2. Weary is each day that comes,
    such ones had not been our way;
  absence from the fian I find
    has turned my mind like one fey.

3. No fairs, no music, no harps,
   no giving of cattle, no deeds with
      horses,
   no rewarding professors with gold,
   no art, no drinking feasts.

3. No music, no harp, no fair,
   no share of wealth, no trained steed,
   no learned men given gold,
   no bold art, no feasts or mead.

4. No love-making, nor hunting—
   the two crafts we had our eyes on—
   no fighting, no making raids,
   no learning, no sports.

4. No wooing, nor hunting chase—
   two crafts we face with heart glad—
   no fight, nor plunder, nor prey,
   no feats or play to be had.

5. Without taking does or deer—
   not like that did I wish it—
   without mention of exploits nor of
      hounds:
   it is long tonight in Oil Finn.

5. No catching of bucks or does—
   not this I chose to begin—
   no word of hounds or delights:
   weary tonight in Oil Finn.

6. Without war gear as usual,
   without playing as was usual for us,
   without swimming with faultless
      champions:
   tonight is long in Oil Finn.

6. No arms nor armor nor games,
   once played on the plains to win;
   no swim with warriors upright:
   weary the night in Oil Finn.

7. My life is long after the Fenians:
   it is fitting it should seem long;
   they were faultless champions:
   it is long tonight in Oil Finn.

7. Since the fian, weary my way;
   fitting to say it grows dim,
   the warriors blameless, upright;
   weary the night in Oil Finn.

8. It is the life as it is for me—
   woe we are so, God,
   I am alone dragging stones—
   it is long tonight in Oil Finn.

8. For the life I lead, my fate,
   God pity the state I am in,
   alone dragging stones my plight:
   weary tonight in Oil Finn.

9. Patrick, for us ask God
   to let it be known the place we will be,
   or will He free my soul from evil?
   It is long tonight in Oil Finn.

9. Patrick, may God let me know
   at what place I must go in,
   or save my soul in sin's spite;
   weary tonight in Oil Finn. Weary.

Meter: 7, throughout; rime 2/4; linking rime or assonance 1/2, 3/4.

## [ 87 ]
# A Grave Marked with Ogam †
*Ogum i llía, lía úas lecht*

Oscar is Oisin's son. Cairpre is the enemy of Finn in the battle of Gabair
(st 5).

1. Ogam on a stone, a stone above a
        grave,
   the place into which men at times
        would go;
   the son of Ireland's king was killed
        there
   by a slim spear above a white horse.

2. Cairpre let fly a fatal throw
   from the back of his horse, good in the
        fray;
   shortly before he met exhaustion,
   Oscar whom his right hand struck down.

3. Oscar let fly a powerful throw,
   angrily, fiercely like a lion,
   and killed Cairpre, grandson of Conn,
   before the champions submitted in
        battle.

4. Keen and tall were the lads
   who found their death from the fight;
   shortly before their arms met
   their dead were more than their living.

5. I myself was in the battle
   on the south side of green Gabair;
   I killed twice fifty warriors;
   it is I who struck them down with my
        hand.

6. I used to play music for a shipman
        under affliction
   when the course was for my destiny;
   I would kill a boar in the sacred wood,
   or I would snatch the egg of the lively
        bird.

7. That ogam there that is on the stone,
   about it fell the doomed;
   were Finn living, champion against
        twenty,
   long would he remember the ogam.

1. Ogam in stone on grave stead,
        where men sometimes tread on course;
   king's son of Ireland cut low,
        hit by spear's throw hurled from horse.

2. Cairpre let a quick cast fly
        from high on horseback, stout steed;
   ere he wearied his hand struck,
        cut down Oscar, cruel deed.

3. Oscar hurled a hard throw, crude,
        like a lion, rude his rage;
   killed Conn's kin, Cairpre proud,
        ere they bowed on battle stage.

4. Tall, keen, cruel were the lads
        who found their death in the strife,
   just before their weapons met;
        more were left in death than life.

5. I myself was in the fight
        on right, south of Gabair green;
   twice fifty warriors I killed,
        my skilled hand slew them, clear,
        clean.

6. I'd play for pirates in bale,
        the while the trail I must tread,
   in holy holt boar I'd fell,
        or would snatch the snell bird's egg.

7. That ogam there in the stone,
        around which the slain fall prone,
   if Finn the fighter could come,
        long would he think on ogam.

Meter: stt 1–6, 7, throughout; st 7, *deibide*; stt 1–6, rime 2/4; stt 1, 3, 5, and
6, linking rime 1/2, 3/4; st 2, linking rime 1/2, linking assonance 3/4; st 4,
linking rime 3/4; st 7, rhythmic rime 1/2.

## [ 88 ]
## Oisin's Dream †
*Tuilsitir mo derca súain*

1. My eyes slept in sleep;
   my spear was near my shield;
   my sword was in my hand,
   and my hand by my ear.

1. Eyes dropping, drowsy with sleep;
   by day shield lay by my spear;
   my sword rested in my hand
   and my hand beneath my ear.

2. A monstrous vision happened to me.
   I let my hounds go swiftly
   at a sow on the plain in order to get
   flesh;
   she happened to be fat to the tusk of
   her jaw.

2. A vast vision came to me:
   my hounds I let swiftly slip
   for flesh of swine on the slope,
   sow's chine abloat to her lip.

3. Thirty paces for me with my shoes,
   on her side to the hair of her nose,
   thirty inches for Finn in her tusk
   above under her skin it is fat.

3. Thirty feet for me with brogues
   to whiskered nose was her side;
   her tusk thirty inches flat
   in upper fat 'neath her hide.

4. Her eye, the size of a cauldron;
   her good lair, the size of a hill.
   My sword sliced her neck,
   and my hound hanging from her ear.

4. Large as a cauldron each eye,
   large as a hill her high lair;
   my sword on her neck cut round
   and my hound on her ear bare.

5. The sow of the eastern Tallann sea
   that beats against the rock that the
   wave strikes;
   for me my limbs were a protection as
   my strength,
   as you are, but not weak like you.

5. From east Tallann the sea swine
   strikes cliffs where brine beats on
   high;
   my limbs, my guard for me strong,
   not weak like you, brawn am I.
   Eyes.

Meter: 7₁ throughout; rime 2/4; st 1, internal rime 3/4; st 2 internal rime 3/4,
linking rime 3/4; stt 3–5 linking rime (sometimes involving one monosyllable
and the first syllable of a two-syllable word) 1/2, 3/4.

## [ 89 ]
## Oisin Remembers Wilder Days
*Ro loiscit no lámasa*

1. These hands have withered;
   these deeds have been checked;
   floodtide has gone, ebb has come,
   and has overwhelmed these powers.

1. Withering hands trembling,
   lingering deeds faltering;
   flood gone, ebb come, waters downed,
   so drowned strength is altering.

2. I thank the Creator,
   that I found profit with high mirth;
   my day in miserable life is long;
   once I was handsome.

2. Thanks to my Lord masterful
   grants joy in deeds dutiful;
       long my day in wretched life—
   once I was blithe, beautiful.

3. I was the best looking of the assembly;
   I found harlots for hire;
   not gently am I journeying from the
        world;
   my impetuous course is done.

3. Viewed in crowds the handsomest,
   I wooed wenches frivolous;
       not feebly I leave the world,
   my course turned from chivalrous.

4. The little pile of pieces that you break
   for this miserable fasting wretch:
   a bit exchange for a stone, a bit for
        bone,
   a bit for this withered hand.

4. The small heap you're severing
   for the weak wretch shriveling:
       from it change some bits for bone,
   for stone, for hand withering.
       Withering.

Meter: 7₃7₃7₁7₃; rime 2/4; internal rime 1/2 (two-syllable rimes); linking rime 3/4.

## [ 90 ]
## Oisin Laments His Youth
*Do bádussa úair*

1. Once I had
   yellow curly hair;
   now come through my head
   only short gray hair.

1. Once I had fine locks,
       yellow, curly, gay;
   now on my head there
       but hair short and gray.

2. I would sooner have
   hair the color of the raven
   coming through my head
   than short gray hair.

2. Better to me were
       locks black like the crow,
   cov'ring my head there
       than short hair like snow.

3. I have no right to woo,
   for I please no women;
   my hair is gray tonight;
   I shall not be as I was.

3. Women I woo not,
       since I now please none;
   my hair tonight—gray;
       what I was is done.

Meter: 5₁ throughout; rime 2/4; linking rime 3/4 (not complete in st 3).

# From the Chronicles

References are to chronicles containing the specific verses, not to persons or battles mentioned.

## { 91 }
## Loch Silenn †
### *Loch Sílend*

Loch Silenn,
woe to him who drinks it on his food!
Cairpre has filled it with heads
so that it is blood reaching to its sand.

Loch Silenn,
  woe to him who drinks its flood
now filled with heads by Cairpre:
  down to sand the lake is blood.

Meter: $3_2 7_1 7_1 7_1$; rime 2/4.
Reference: *AI* 573.

## { 92 }
## Ainmire mac Setna †
### *Femen in tan ro boí rí*

Femen when there was a king
was not a spot that was not brave;
today its color is bright red
by (the hand of) Ainmire son of Setna.

Femen, as long as kings led,
  nowhere was valor wanted;
today its hue crimson red
  by Ainmire undaunted.

Meter: $7_1 7_2 7_1 7_2$; rime 1/3, 2/4.
References: *AU* 575, *CS* 569, *Tig.*, *RC* 17.148.

## [ 93 ]
# His Queen Laments Aed Son of Ainmire
*Batar inmuine in trí toíb*

Dear were the three sides
to which I do not expect a return:
the little side of Tara, the side of Tailltiu,
the side of Aed son of Ainmire.

Belovèd were the three sides—
no return for me again:
sides of Tara, of Teltown,
of Aed—none I'll see again.

Meter: 7₁7₃7₂7₃; rime 2/4.
References: *CS* 598, *FM* 595.

## [ 94 ]
# On the Death of Aed mac Colgan, King of Airther
*Ro boí tan*

1. There was a time
   when Loch Da Dam was a pool of
   　　excellence,
   it was not the lake that was splendid,
   but chief Aed son of Colgan.

1. On a time
   Loch Da Dam was proud and fine;
   not for the loch its splendor,
   but for Aed its defender.

2. It is all the same to me,
   since the friend who loved me does not
   　　live,
   whoever should put a wattled house
   on the island of Loch Da Dam.

2. No care mine,
   since loved friend died, the decline
   of the isle in Loch Da Dam,
   though humble hut there some time.

Meter: st 1, 3₁7₁7₂7₂, rime 1/2, 3/4 (*deibide* with rhythmic rimes); st 2, 3₁7₁7₁7₁,
rime 1/2/4 with 3 consonating.
References: *FM* 606, *CS* 610, *Tig.*, *RC* 17.168–169.

## [ 95 ]
# The Drowning of Conaing
*Tonna mora mórglana*

1. The great clear waves of the sea
   and the sand they covered
   flung themselves together on Conaing
   into his weak wicker coracle.

1. Wild wet waves are billowing
   across sea-sands thundering
   setting on Conaing alone
   in his frail craft sundering.

2. The woman threw her white mane
   at Conaing in his coracle;

2. The hag her white mane lets fling
   at Conaing's curach sinking;

| | |
|---|---|
| she smiles a twisted smile | a cruel grin curls her lip |
| today toward the sacred tree of Tortu. | at Tortu tree, the magic. |

Meter: st 1, 7₃7₃7₁7₃, rime 2/4, much alliteration; st 2, *deibide*.
References: *AU* 621, *CS* 622, *Tig.*, *RC* 17.175–176.

## [ 96 ]
## On the Death of Mael Fothartaig †
*Ní diliu*

| | |
|---|---|
| Not dearer | No dearer |
| is any king than another to me, | is one king than another, |
| since Mael Fothartaig was carried | since they brought Mael Fothartaig |
| in his cerecloth to Derry. | to Derry 'neath cere cover. |

Meter: 3₂7₂7₃7₂; rime 2/4; consonance 1/2.
References: *AU* 668, *FM* 668.

## [ 97 ]
## On the Death of Aed mac Colgan,
## King of Leinster †
*Int Áed issin úir*

| | |
|---|---|
| That Aed in the ground | That Aed in the ground, |
| the king in the burial place | the king in the tomb, |
| the little bird—dear, pure— | that dainty dear one |
| with St. Ciaran in Clonmacnois. | with Ciaran in Cloon. |

Meter: 5₁ throughout; rime 2/4; consonance all endings; internal rime 3/4.
References: *FM* 734, *AIr:frag.* 3.695.

## [ 98 ]
## Cuchuimne †
*Cuchuimne*

| | |
|---|---|
| 1. Cuchuimne | 1. Cuchuimne |
| read half of knowledge; | studied half of lore duly; |
| the other half to be sought | half he should be seeking for, |
| he left for women. | left for wenches—fleeting lore. |
| 2. Well for Cuchuimne as he was, | 2. Well for Cuchuimne, the praised; |
| when that passed away he became wise; | that passed, he became a sage; |

he left women in neglect;                    he left wenches and progressed,
he read the rest while he had life.          then read the rest in his age.

Meter: st 1, *deibide* with rhythmic rimes; st 2, 7, throughout, rime 1/2/4, linking rime 3/4.
References: *AU* 746, *FM* 742.

## [ 99 ]
## The Drowning of Niall Son of Aed †
### *Mallacht ort, a Challainn chrúaid*

1. A curse on you, harsh Callann
   its stream like mist of a mountain;
   it brought early death on every side
   on the warlike, shining face of dark
   Niall.

1. Curse you, Callann, harsh your stream,
   mountain mist its flood of foam;
   death on every side brought down,
   and on Niall's brown, brave brow
   shown.

2. I do not love the ill-omened water
   that flows beside my house;
   Callann, though you boast of it,
   the son of a tender mother you have
   drowned.

2. I loathe the dire river Callann
   that flows beside my dwelling;
   loved mother weeps son's drowning,
   sounding flood boasts his knelling.

Meter: st 1, 7, throughout, rime 2/4, linking rime 1/2, 3/4, frequent alliteration; st 2, 8₂6₂7₂7₂, rime 2/4, consonance 1/2, linking rime 3/4. The irregularity of the syllabic length of lines suggests the meter in st 2 may be accentual and not syllabic. Very likely the second stanza is the older, for only it appears in *AU*.
References: *AU* 845, *FM* 844.

## [ 100 ]
## Kenneth Son of Conaing Is Executed by Drowning †
### *Monúar a doine maithi*

*FM* and *CS* (which does not contain the poem) give the following note: "Cinnaedh, son of Conaing, kin of Cianachta, was drowned in a pool, a cruel death, by Maelsechnaill and Tigernach, with the approval of the good men of Ireland, and of the successor of Patrick especially." Only *FM* gives the second stanza.

1. Alas, good people,
   better were his days of sport;
   great woe that Kenneth son of Conaing
   was in bonds [brought] to the pool.

1. Alas, good folk, I'm saying
   his playing days were better;
   Conaing's son Kenneth's slaughter
   in pool water, bound by fetter.

2. After mangling him in the sea,
   great is the sorrow that the army suffers
   seeing his white rib-cage
   on the strand above the cold river
       Ainge.

2. Since mangling him in the sea,
       great grief overwhelms the host
   looking on his white ribs rolled
       where cold Ainge meets the coast.

Meter: st 1, 7₂ throughout, rime 2/4, consonance 1/2/4, linking rime 1/2, 3/4; st 2, 7₁ throughout, rime 2/4, consonance 1/2/3/4, assonance 1/2, linking rime 3/4.
References: *AU 850, FM 849.*

## [ 101 ]
# Death of Princes †
### *Rúaidri Manann minn n-áine*

1. Ruadri of Man, a crown of splendor,
   Aed from the borders of Cantyre;
   Donnchad, fair one fit to be a prince,
   Garbsith, gentle gem of Macha.

1. Manx Ruaidri, crown of splendor;
       Aed from far Cantyre's corner;
   fair Donnchad, fit for ruler;
       Garbsith, Macha's adorner.

2. When it comes to my notice
   most sharp are the farthest corners of
       my heart;
   cold flagstones after guarding
   where our white-topped heroes were.

2. When these I heed, regarding,
       harsh hurt to my heart's hollow;
   cold stones now after guarding
       where hardened heroes follow.

Meter: 7₂ throughout; st 1, rime 2/4, all endings consonate; st 2, rime 1/3 (rime riche), 2/4, linking rime 3/4.
References: *AU 877.*

# Appendix

IRISH TEXT OF POEMS
NOT IN RECENT COLLECTIONS

[Spelling normalized to a thirteenth-century standard except in nos. 53
and 86, which reproduce the spelling of the fifteenth-century manuscripts.]

## [ 5 ]
## Calendar of the Birds

1. Énlaith betha bríg cen táir
   is ar fáilti frisin gréin;
   hi noin enáir cipsi úair,
      congair a slúaig din chaill chéir.

2. I n-ocht calaind apréil áin
   tecait fainnli na firdáil;
      traig ardibig cid nosceil
      o ocht calaind octimbir.

3. I féil Rúadáin rád cen diss
   is and osclaicther a nglaiss;
   hi sechtmad déc calaind mái,
      dogair in chái din chaill chaiss.

4. I Tamlachti anait éoin
      do chantain chíuil hi noin Iúil
   do Mail Rúain, ná ruc Badb [dí]
      co n-aitchet bí [i] laithi[u] liúin.

5. I féil Cíarain meic in tsaer
      tic giugrainn dar fairge úar;
   i féil Ciprian condelgg n-oll
      géisid dam donn din rái rúad.

6. Trí fichit cet mblíadna mbán,
      amser in domuin cen lén;
   memais trethan dar cach n-airm,
      i ndíaid aidchi im gairm na n-én.

7. Atnagat combinni cheóil
      ind éoin fri Ríg nime nél
   ic admolad ind Ríg réil
      coistid do chéin cleir na n-én.

## [ 9 ]
## Winter Has Come

Táinic gaimred co ngainni,
rolínsat lethe linni,
      arlegat duile degnad,
      rogab tonn medrach minni.

## [ 13 ]
## The Worst and Best Weather

Hed is annsam do rímaib:
fleochud, snechta co sirgail;
      in drucht is in grian glan glé
      is ed as dech sonenne.

## [ 14 ]
## Slieve Cua

Slíab cúa cúanach corrach dub
  glaid gaeth ima glinni
    gairit 'ma cluichthe;
becid borbdam banodur
  isin fagomur uime;
    éigid corr os a cluichthe.

## [ 26 ]
## Alone by Choice

Glé limsa, a Choimdiu cen chol,
  bethu bocht is bith m'oenor
ropad glé limsa dom déoin
  ingnais mo cháem, mo chenéoil.

## [ 31 ]
## Prayers to Save and Shelter

Cid lúath cach gadur glan glé
  oc tafann fíada ar bith cé,
    is lúaithi in irnaigthi sunn
  oc tabairt anma a hifurn.

2. Gér imda éigem isin chath
  oc feraib Éirenn ar Muig Rath,
    as lía a n-ifirn fó thrí
    'ca orgain don irnigthi.

3. Sír-gabail na salm fa sech
  ocus Bíaiti na cléirech,
    oc demnaib as mór a fúath
    cid mall gabthar no cid lúath.

## [ 32 ]
## Hymn to Saint Brigit

1. Brigit bé bithmaith
    breó órde óiblech,
  donfé don bithflaith
    in grén tind tóidlech.

2. Ronsóira Brigit
    sech drungu demne:
  roróina reunn
    cathu cach thedme.

3. Dirodba indiunn
    ar colno císu
  in chróib co mbláthib
    in máthir Ísu.

4. Ind fíróg inmain
    co n-orddon adbil,
  bé sóir cech inbaid
    lam nóib di Laignib.

5. Lethcholbe flatho
    la Patricc prímde
  in tlacht ós lígib
    ind rígin rígde.

6. Robet er sinit
    ar cuirp hi cilicc;
  dia rath ronbróina
    ronsóira Brigit.

## [ 35 ]
## Who Knows of His Death?

In ba maiten, in ba fuin,
in ba for úr no for muir,
  acht ro fetar rachad d'éc;
mór in bét ni fetar cuin.

## [ 36 ]
## Mo Ling Offends None

Tan bím eter mo sruithe
am teist ergaire cluiche;
  tan bím eter in n-áes mer
  do-muinet is mé a n-óiser.

## [ 41 ]
## Colum Cille in Exile

1. Mellach lem bith i n-ucht ailiun
     for beind cairrge,
   co n-aicind and ar a menci
     féth na fairrge.

2. Co n-aicind a tonda troma
     úas ler lethan,
   amail canait ceól dia n-Athair
     for seól bethad.

3. Co n-aicind a trácht réid rindglan,
     ní dál dubai,
   co cloisind guth na n-én n-ingnad,
     seól co subai.

4. Co cloisind torm na tond tana
     forsna cairrge,
   co cloisind, núall ri táeb reilcci,
     fúam na fairrge.

5. Co n-aicind a helta ána
     ós lir lindmar,
   co n-aicind na míla mara,
     mó cech n-ingnad.

6. Co n-aicind a tráig 's a tuli
     ina réimim;
   co mbad hé m'ainm, rún no ráidim,
     "Cúl fri hÉirinn."

7. Co n-am-tísad congain cride
     ic a fégad;
   co rocóinind m'ulcu ile,
     annsa a rélad.

8. Co robennachainn in Coimdid
     conic huile,
   nem co muintir gráid co nglaine,
     tír, tráig, tuile.

9. Co roscrútainn óen na lebar,
     maith dom anmain,
   sel for sléchtain ar nem n-inmain,
     sel for salmaib.

10. Sel ic scrútain flatha nime,
      náemda in cennach;
    sel for sáethar ná bad forrach,
      ropad mellach.

11. Sel ic búain duilisc do charraic,
      sel ic aclaid,
    sel ic tabairt bid do bochtaib,
      sel i ccarcair.

12. In comairle is ferr fíad Día
      dam nostenda,
    ním-reilge an Rí díanam gilla,
      ní nom-mella!

## [ 43 ]
## Colum Cille and Guaire

1. Déna, a Gúaire, maith um ní,
     na seóit do-chí as dorn im ceó:
   at oenar tánaic tú a clí,
     do-géba ní an fat bía beó.

2. Scáil, a maic Colmáin, do crad
     is búaine blad iná seóit:
   intí da tabair Día ní,
     ní maith rí 'sa beth co neóit.

3. A degmic Colmáin na clíar,
     mo chen is fíal, mairg is gann,
   ná cuir sed 'san saegul sunn,
     's gan acht sel cach oeinfir ann.

4. Rígrad domain, cuma n-éc,
     muna bronnat sét is bíad
   muna chosnat féin a mblad,
     ní téit ar nem fer dúr, dían.

5. Is mé Colum Cille cáid
     bec do commus am láim féin:
   ón ló fa tánac a clí,
     ní dernus acht do deóin Dé.

## [ 44 ]
## Guaire and Marban

GUAIRE

1. A Marbáin, a díthrubaig,
   cid ná cotlai for colcaid?
   Ba meinciu duit feiss i-mmaig,
   cenn do raig for lár ochtgaig.

MARBAN

2. Nicon cotlaim for colcaid,
   cía bether com imslánud:
   atáid sochaidi i-mmaig
   atraig úaim imrádud.

3. Ní marait ar comolta,
   scarad friu nín lúaidi:
   acht mad óinsessior namá
   ní mair nech díb, a Gúaire.

4. Ornait ocus Lugna lán.
   Laidgen ocus Ailirán,
   (atá cecht urde fri dán,)
   Marbán ocus Cluithnechán.

5. Ro chluinis mo tiomna-sa
   fri úair techta don domun:
   mo cúach-sa din díthrebach,
   mo chráin do Laidgen lobur.

6. Mo scían is mo srethugad,
   mo trebad i Túaim Aidchi,
   mo lorg, mo crain, mo cúach,
   mo tíag lethoir, mo cairchi.

GUAIRE

7. A Marbáin, a díthrubaig,
   cid dia timna do chúach?
   di don fiur cerda a rath,
   acht a brath do Mac Dúach.

## [ 53 ]
## Loveloneliness

1. Och is fada atáim a-muigh
   ón duine ara bfuil mo grádh,
   gion go fognann si mar breith
   faide liom ná leis gach lá.

2. Uime ní fuilim go fúar
   gion gur búan orom a gean,
   dá innsi ní rac[h]a mé
   mas bean é mas [í] fear.

3. Mé is no c[h]ompán go bráth,
   ní cuirfeam ar grádh [go foth]
   gid bé hí nó gid bé hé,
   oc[hán], a Dé, oc[h]án och!

## [ 57 ]
## A Splendid Sword

Luin oc elaib,
ungi oc dírnaib,
delba* ban n-aithech
oc ródaib rígnaib,
ríg oc Domnall,
dord oc aidbse,
adand oc caindill:
calg oc mo chailg-se.

## [ 58 ]
## The Necessity of Reading

Cid glic fri hailchi úara,
cid saer ac imirt béla,
cid binn a dord fri dúana,
do chúala as borb nat léga.

*Suggested by Thurneysen for alliteration;
ms. has *crotha.*

[ 59 ]
## You See Your Own Faults In Others

Cid becc—mét friget—do locht,
airige for nech do chéin;
cid métither slíab do locht,
nocha n-airige fort féin.

[ 63 ]
## Fann's Farewell to Cu Chulainn

1. Fégaid mac láechraidi Lir
   Do maigib Éogain Inbir:
   Manannán úas domun dind
   ro boí tan rop inmain lim.

2. Mád indíu bá dígrais núall,
   ní charand mo menma múad:
   is éraise in rét int serc:
   téit a héol cen immitecht.

3. Lá ro bása ocus mac Lir
   hi ngríanán Dúni Inbir,
   ropo dóig lind cen anad
   noco bíad ar n-imscarad.

4. Dánam thuc Manannán mass
   robam céle comadas:
   noco bérad orm ria lind
   cluchi eráil ar fidchill.

5. Dánam thuc Manannán mass
   robam céle comadas:
   dornasc d'ór aromthá
   thuc dam i llúag m'imdergthá.

6. Baí acum dar fráech immach
   cóeca ingen illdathach:
   doratus dó cóecait fer
   centar in chóecat ingen.

7. Cethra cóecait cen miri
   iss é lucht inn óentigi,
   dá chóecait fer sónmech slán,
   dá chóecait ban find follán.

8. Atchíu dar in muir i lle—
   nín acend nach meraige—
   marcach in mara mongaig:
   ní lenand do sithlongaib.

9. T'imthecht seochainni co se
   ní acend acht sídaige:
   máraid do chíall cech slúag séim,
   cía beit úait i n-etercéin.

10. Mad messe bá dethbir dam,
    dáig at báetha cíalla ban:
    intí ro charus co holl
    domrat sund i n-écomlond.

11. Celebrad dit, a Chú chain!
    Aso sind úait co sochraid.
    Cén co tísam dúthracht lind:
    is ard cech recht co himchim.

12. Érge seo mithig damsa:
    atá nech risnid andsa:
    is mór in tóchosol trá,
    a Laíg, a meic Ríangabrá.

13. Ragat rim chéli fodéin,
    dág noco dingnea m'amréir:
    nár apraid is céim i cleith:
    mád álic dúibsi fégaid.

[ 65 ]
## The Snow Is Cold Tonight

1. In-nocht is fúar in snechta,
   fodechta is búan mo bochta,
   nidom neirt isin debaid,
   im geilt rom-geoguin gorta.

2. At-chid cach nidom chuchtach,
   is lom i snáth mo cheirtech,
   Suibne m'ainm o Ros Ercain,
   is misi in geltán geltach.

3. Nidom fois o thic agaid,
    ní thaidlenn mo chois conair,
    nacha bíu sonna a ccíana
    dom-eccat íalla omain.

4. Mo báire tar muir mbarcláin
    ar ndol tar sáile soclán,
    rogab time mo nertán,
    is me geltán Glinne Bolcáin.

5. Gáeth in reoid oc mo rébad,
    snechta rom-león co leicce,
    int síon dom breith i n-éccaib
    do géccaib cacha geicce.

6. Rom-gonsat gécca glasa
    coro rébsat mo bossa,
    ní fargaibset na dresa
    damna cresa dom chossa.

7. Atá crith ar mo láma
    tar cach mbith fátha mbúaidre,
    do Sléib Mis ar Slíab Cuillenn,
    do Sléib Cuillenn co Cúailgne.

8. Is trúag mo núallán choidche
    i mullach Crúachán Oigle,
    do Glinn Bolcáin for Íle,
    do Chinn Tíre for Boirche.

9. Bec mo chuit ó thig laa,
    ní tháet ar scáth lá noa,
    barr biorair Chlúana Cille
    la gléorán Chille Cúa.

10. In gen fil ag Ros Ercach
    ní thair imned ná olcach,
    as ed dombeir cen nerta
    beith re snechta co nochtach.

## [ 66 ]
## My Night in Cell Derfile

1. M'agaid i cCill Derffile
    is í robris mo chride,
    dursan dam, a mic mo Dé,
    scarad re Dal nAraidé.

2. Deichnemar is deich cet láoch
    rob é mo slúag ac Druim Fraoch,
    cía beó cen treisi, a mic Dé,
    ba misi i ccenn comairlé.

3. Muichnide m'agaid in-nocht
    cen gilla is cen longphort,
    nirb í m'agaid oc Druim Dam,
    meisi is Faolchú is Congal.

4. Mairg romfuirged risin dáil,
    a mo ruire an ríchid ráin,
    cen co bfagainn-si d'ulc de
    co bráth acht in oidchi-se.

## [ 67 ]
## The Woman
## Who Reaps the Watercress

1. A ben benus a birar
    ocus berius in uisci,
    nocha betheá cen ní in-nocht
    cen co mbertheá mo chuit-si.

2. Monúarán, a benacán,
    nocha raga in leth ragat,
    misi im-muig a mbarraib crann,
    túsa tall i tig charat.

3. Monúarán, a benacán,
    is fúar in gáeth dom-anuic
    ním-orchis mathair na mac,
    ní fuil brat ar mo braiguit.

4. Dá festá-sa, a benacán,
    mar atá sunna Suibne,
    sech ní fagaid cuibde neich,
    ní fagaid nech a chuibde.

5. Ní théigim a n-oirechtus
    etir ócuib mo thíre,
    ní déntar dam oinechtres,
    ní théit m'aire re ríge.

6. Ní théigim ar aeididecht
    do thig mic duine i nÉire,
    fa meince lim báeithgeltacht
    ar bennuib corra sléibe.

7. Ní tecar dom airfitiud
    athaig re ndul im ligi,
    nochan faguim oirchisecht
    ó fer túaithe ná fini.

8. Intan ropsom Suibni-si
    ocus théigim ar echaib,
    intan tic im chuimni-si
    mairg rom-fuirced i mbethaid.

9. Is mé Suibne sáeirchendaid,
    is úar anoíbinn m'inad,
    cía béo in-nocht ar baithbendaib
    a ben benus mo birar.

10. Is é mo mid m'uisci fúar,
    is é mo búar mo birar,
    is íad mo charait mo chrainn,
    cía 'tú cen lenn, cen inar.

11. Is úar in-nocht in adaig,
    cid im bocht ar áei mbirair,
    at-chúala guth in giogruinn
    ós Imlig imluim Ibair.

12. Atú cen brat, cen inar,
    fata a ulc úair rom-lenad,
    teichim re guth na cuirre
    mar bud buille rom-benad.

13. Ricim co Dairbre ndaingen
    isna láib aidblib erraig,
    ocus teichim re n-oidche
    síar co Boirche mbennaig.

14. Diamsat eólach, a finngág,
    mo gort ní treórach tenngarg,
    atá nech dianad sceile
    in t-eiri beri, a bengág.

15. It úara dotachuisin
    ar brú topair glais grenaig,
    deog gleórda d'uisci idan
    ocus a birar benaid.

16. Mo chuit-si in birar benaid
    cuit geilte sáeire singi
    scingid gáeth úar 'mam rennaib
    do bennaib cacha binni.

17. Is úar gáeth in matanraid,
    do-icc etrom is m'inar,
    nachan fétaim t'acallaim,
    a ben benus a mbirar.

IN BEN

18. Fágaib mo chuit don Choimdi,
    rium-sa ná déna duilge,
    móite fo-geba cennacht,
    is beir bennacht, a Suibne.

SUIBNE

19. Dénam cennach cert cubaid
    cía 'tú a mullach in iubair,
    beir m'inar is mo chertín,
    fágaib in mbertín mbirair.

20. Is terc nech las am inmuin,
    ní fuil mo thech ar talmain,
    uaim ó bere mo birar
    mo chuit chinad ar th'anmain.

21. Ní ris a nech ro-charais,
    meisti don tí ro-lenais,
    ro-fágbuis nech co daidbir
    imon airbir ro-benais.

22. Crech na nGall ngorm dot gabáil,
    orm nocha dernais degdáil,
    co bfagba on Choimde a chinaid
    mo chuit birair do benáil.

23. A ben, chugut da ttóra
    Loingsechan atá rún reba
    tabair-si dó trem chinaid
    a leth in birair bena.

## { 69 }
## The Cursed Banquet

1. "In chuit sin chaithise in-nocht,
   cen úabar, cen imarnocht:
      og circe ón ríg nársat car,
      is og géoid do Máelodar.

2. "Nochan fitir misi ríam,
   comad úasal ríg Oirgíall,
      noco faca in Máelodar,
      i tig óil 'cá fíadugad.

3. "Dá mbeith oc óenríg cen ail,
   cenél Conaill is Eógain.
      is Oirgíalla fri gním nga,
      nír dulta dó a t'inadsa.

4. "In chuit sin co teilged gaill,
   tucad duit i tig Domnall,"
      ar Gair Gann, "nárub slán duit
      má dá toimli tú in drochchuit."

## { 73 }
## Grainne's Forest Fare

Is maith do chuit, a Gráinne,
   is ferr duit inda ríge:
sercoll na cailech feda
   la banna meda míne.

## { 75 }
## Caeilte Speaks of Finn

Dámad ór in duille donn
   chuires di in chaill,
dámad airget in gel tonn
   ro thidlaicfed Finn.

## { 76 }
## Arran

1. Arann na n-aiged n-imda,
      tadall fairce rea formna,
   ailén i mbíadta buidne,
      druimne i ndergthar gaí gorma.

2. Aige baetha ara bennaib,
      mónainn maetha 'na mongaib,
   uisce úar ina haibnib,
      mes ara dairgib donnaib.

3. Mílchoin innti is gagair,
      sméra is airne dub droigin,
   dlúith a fraig rena fedaib,
      daim oc dedail 'má doirib.

4. Díglaim corcra ara cairrcib,
      fér cen locht ara lercaib,
   ósa crecaib, caem cumtaig,
      surdgail laeg mbrecc oc bedcaig.

5. Mín a mag, méth a muca,
      súairc a guirt, scél as chreitte,
   cno for barraib a fidcholl,
      seólad na sithlong seicce.

6. Aíbinn dóib ó thicc soinenn,
      bricc fá brúachaib a habann,
   frecrait faílinn 'má finnall,
      aíbinn cech inam Arann.

## { 77 }
## Well of the Strand of Two Women

1. A thopair Trága Dá Ban,
   álainn do bilar barrglan:
      ó ro tréiced do chnúas ort
      nír léiced fás dot fochlocht.

2. Do bricc ód brúachaib immach,
   do mucca allta it fásach,
   daim do chreca, caín selca,
   do laíg brecca broinnderca.

3. Do mes ós barraib do chrann,
   t'íasc i n-inberaib th'abann:
   álainn lí do gas ngegair,
   a glas úaine foithremail.

4. Is úait do-chúatar in Fíann
   dár marbad Coinchenn coimfíal,
   dár cuired ár Féinne Finn
   isin matain ós Maelglinn.

5. Úait do-chúaid Fatha na fled,
   ba laech do fuilnged imned,
   dá fúair rath in talman tair,
   dár marbad i cath Chláraig.

6. Táinic ós cinn in topair
   Blaí ingen Deirc Díanscothaig:
   gol ard cona nath aicce
   dár cuired cath Confaite.

7. Ar marbad con ocus fer,
   ar n-athchumma laech lángel,
   co cúala glaed Garaid glain
   adaig re taeb in topair.

[ 78 ]
## The Sons of Lugaid

1. Trí tuile
   ticed a dún Ard Ruide:
   tuile ócán, tuile ech,
   tuile mílchon mac Luigdech.

2. Trí ceóla
   oc rígaib ségda ar sodain;
   ceól crot, ceól timpán co mblaid,
   dord Fir Thuinne meic Throgain.

3. Trí gáire
   bít ann cen úair fo therca;
   gáir chetnat fora faithche,
   gáir graifne ocus gáir erca.

4. Trí gáire:
   gáir a muc ndrónnmar ndega,
   gáir á slúaig ós blía bruidne,
   gáir muirne is gáir meda.

5. Trí cnúasa
   bítis ann úas a slattaib;
   cnúas oc tuitim, foram ngnáth,
   cnúas fo bláth is cnúas apaig.

6. Trí meic forácaib Lugaid
   cérsat rulaid a fedma;
   Ruide mac Luidech lethain,
   Echaid is Fíacha ferda.

7. Do-bér-sa teist ar Echaid
   ná dechaid traigid madma:
   nocha n-epert guth bad ró,
   ní bíd bad mó bad calma.

8. Do-bér-sa teist ar Fíachaid
   cérsat rulaid a fogla:
   ní bíd cen airfited gnáth,
   ní bíd tráth cen ól corma.

9. Do-bér-sa teist ar Ruide,
   cos' tictis na trí tuile,
   nár ér nech Ruide im ní ríam
   ocus nár íarr ní ar duine.

10. Trícha ruirech, trícha tríath,
    trícha nía, ba foram rí,
    ba hé lín a slúaig chétaig
    trícha do chétaib fa thrí.

[ 80 ]
## Beagles Bay
## on the Hill of Kings

1. Guth gadair i cCnoc na Ríg:
   inmain lim in síd foa ffuil;
   ba meince leinn fulacht fían
   etir in slíab ocus muir.

2. Innso báttar teglach Finn,
   gasraid ler binn gotha tét;
   inmain limsa in buiden mer
   do théiged ar fecht mór ccét.

3. Dar leinn ba sochraid a selg;
   mór ndam nderg do thuit lea n-ág;
   imda cú dath-ballach dían
   'sa slíab oc techt ina ndál.

4. Bran ocus Sceólang co scéim
   a choin féin i láim in ríg;
   ba hinmain le Finn na coin;
   ba maith a ngoil is a ngním.

5. Cnú Deireóil i n-ucht in ríg,
   degmac Loga fa cáem cruth,
   ro baí oc seinm cruiti d'Fionn,
   in fer fion dobad mór guth.

6. Cach toíssech nónbur don féin
   do thiged féin 'chum in ríg
   do commorad na selg mór
   do níd in slóg fa Druim Chaín.

7. Coeca dam co n-imad mbenn
   do thuitset lem féin, a rí,
   ar óen is coeca torc,
   acht cia ataim in-nocht cen ní.

8. Longphort oc clainn Ronáin rúaid
   ar in táeb so thúaid don glenn;
   ba sochraid oc fulacht fían
   do-gníod in Fían i mbonaib benn.

9. Clanna Morna fa buiden mer
   co n-imad fer don taíb thes,
   minic do chuirtis gleó crúaid
   is do thictis fa búaid as.

10. Do-chúala guth gadair deirg
    ar in leirg láim ris in sruth;
    do-thógaib tonna mo chinn,
    faíd in gadair is binn guth.

11. Is mé Oisín mac in ríg;
    is fata ó do-chrín mo cruth;
    cia atá mo chroidi teinn,
    nocha linn nach binn in guth.

[ 81 ]
## A Bell Rings on the Red Ridge

OISIN
1. Faíd cluic do-chúala i nDruim Deirg
   mar a ndéntis in Fían seilg;
   ní chúala ríam roime soin
   guth cluic i fforaís fíadaig.

PATRICK
2. Faíd cluic do-chúala i nDruim Deirg
   mar a ndéntis in Fían seilg;
   ocus ní cúala rem ré
   óenguth ann bud binné.

OISIN
3. Faíd cluic do-chúala i nDruim Deirg
   mar a ndéntis in Fían seilg;
   binne lim ar techt ar slóg
   in dord Fían 'ca ttinól.

4. Faíd cluic do-chúala i nDruim Deirg
   mar a ndéntis in Fían seilg;
   binne lim ar ttecht immach
   in fet do-gníd mac Lugach.

5. Annam le coill Droma Deirg
   faíd cluic innti leirg do leirg;
   ba mince don ál chúaine
   deired oidche adfúaire.

6. Cía in trú chleirigso síar
   benus a chluicín co dían;
      nach eistinn re guth na ccon
      ata'sa glinn 'na forrad.

PATRICK

7. Cid binn letsa guth na ccon,
   ocus cid adbar menman,
      is binne leisin Ríg in nech
      eistes comrád na ccleirech.

OISIN

8. Cid binn letsa a n-abrait soin,
   ocus cid maith let menmain,
      is binne buirech in daim mir
      no in ceól chanait na cleirig.

9. Ad-connarcsa fir 'sa muig,
   nac eistfed re guth do cluig,
      is do fuicfed marb ma-le
      tusa is do cleirig uile.

10. Binne lim um trath eirge
    cerca fraích i mbennaib sléibe,
       no guth in cleirig istaig
       oc meiglig oc meigellaig.

PATRICK

11. A Oisín innis scéla
    is na leig sinn fo méla;
       crét do-déntis rimsa de
       fan cluigínso benaimse?

OISIN

12. Do-beirimsi bríatar co fír,
    luigim fo anmain mo ríg,
       co mbenfad do cloc it cenn
       noco mbeitheá cen anam.

13. Da ccluined Garb Doire dían
    faíd cluic 'sa chillso síar,
       do rachad co grot istech
       's do brisfed cloc na ccleirech.

14. Da ccluined Finn in féindid
    faíd do cluigín a chleirig
       do rachad it cenn cen acht,
       is ní ro-icfed úait imtecht.

15. Da ccluined Conán na fFían
    faíd in cluicsi rim aníar
       cleirig betha do beith ann,
       do beitís uile cen anam.

16. Da ccluined Caílti croide,
    fer nar opthach n-irgaile,
       do rachad istech cen gaí
       's do brisfed bar ccluiginí.

17. Uchán is crad lem chroide
    scarad re leirg Máenmoige,
       is rissin láechraid ffeilsin
       rem féin is rem degeicsib.

18. Is me Oisín degmac Finn,
    creidim Día thúas a Thailcinn;
       cia atu in-nocht cen féin cen maín,
       is pían lim faíd in chluigín.

[ 82 ]

# The Death
# of Finn's Hound Conbecc

1. Trúag lem aided Chonbicce
      Conbecc ba lór a glaine;
   ní faca bad chroibglicce
      i ndíaid muicce ná aige.

2. Saeth lem aided Chonbicce,
      Conbecc in gotha gairge;
   ní faca bad chroibglicce
      oc marbad daim cen cairde.

3. Saeth lem aided Chonbicce
      ós tonnaib arda úaine;
   a aided ba chomraime,
      a bás ba lór a thrúaige.

## { 83 }
## Caeilte Sang of Strength Departed

1. Bec in-nocht lúth mo dá lúa,
   ro fetar mo chorp is cúa:
   ropo maith rith adám renn
   noco tóracht in Tálcenn.

2. Ropsa chrib mo dá ulaig,
   adám áed im' chalb culaig,
   adám braicc conbíatais baidb,
   nirpsat m'airm-si can ulaig.

3. Ra luidinn-se de marcaib,
   ar argg níad ropsam fortail,
   do-berinn culu ar gart Finn,
   ropsam grinn grinn ri harcaib.

4. Missi is Oissín mac Finn,
   ropsat comchuibde ar ceta,
   ar ngníma ropsat mára,
   ar mbága rapsat beca.

Glosses in ms.: 1.1 mo dá choiss. 1.3 mo dám
choss. 1.4 Patric. 2.1 mo dá choiss. 2.2 adám súil
im chinn cométsat. 2.3 adám lám. 3.2 láech
trénfer. 3.3 comét ar einech. 3.4 ri harccib.

## { 85 }
## Music of the World

1. Binn guth duine i dTír in Óir,
   binn in glór chanait na h-eóin;
   binn in núallán do-gní in chorr,
   binn in tonn i mBun Dá Threóir.

2. Binn in fogar do-gní in gaeth,
   binn guth cúach ós Caise Con
   álainn dellrad do-gní grían,
   binn aníar fetgail na lon.

3. Binn guth iolair Easa Rúaid
   ós cionn Cúain Mic Morna móir;
   binn guth cúach ós barraib dos,
   álainn in tost do-gní in chorr.

4. Finn mac Cumaill m'athair féin,
   secht ccatha 'na féin co grinn;
   in úair léicmís coin ré fíad,
   a ngáir ina díaid bud binn.

## { 86 }
## A Dreary Night in Elphin

1. Is fada anocht i n-Oil Finn,
   fada linn an oidhche a-réir;
   an lá i-niu gidh fada dhamh,
   do ba leór fad an laoi i-né.

2. Fada liom gach lá dá dtig;
   ní mar sin ba cleachtadh dhún;
   mo bheith i n-éagmhais na bhFian,
   do chuir sin mo chiall ar gcúl.

3. Gan aonach, gan cheól, gan chruit,
   gan bronnadh cruidh, gan gníomh
      greagh,
   gan díol ollamhan ar ór,
   gan ealadhain, gan ól fleadh.

4. Gan bheith ag suirghe ńa ag seilg—
   an dá cheird le a raibh ar súil—
   gan deabhaidh, gan déanamh creach,
   gan bheith ag foghlaim chleas lúith.

5. Gan bhreith ar eilid ná ar fiadh,
   ní h-amhlaidh sin budh mhian linn,
   gan luadh ar coinbheirt ná ar coin:
   is fada anocht i nOil Finn.

6. Gan earradh gaisgidh do ghnáth,
   gan imirt mar badh ál linn
   gan snámh re laochraidh ar loch,—
   is fada a-nocht i nOil Finn.

7. Fada ar saoghal d'éis na bhFian;
   ní cneasta ná badh cian linn;
   fá hiad an laochradh gan locht;
   is fada a-nocht i nOil Finn.

8. Is don tsaoghal mar tá mé;
   is truagh, a Dhé! mar tá sinn,
   im aonar ag tarraing chloch;
   is fada a-nocht i nOil Finn.

9. Sir, a Phádraig, dhuinn ar Dhia
   fios an ionaidh a mbia sinn,
   nó an saorfa m'anam ar olc;
   is fada a-nocht i nOil Finn!

## [ 87 ]
## A Grave Marked with Ogam

1. Ogum i llía, lía úas lecht,
   baile i téigtis fecht fir;
   mac ríg Érenn ro gáet ann,
   do gae gann os gabur gil.

2. Tarlaic Cairpre airchur n-airc
   do muin a mairc maith is tress;
   gair siu condristais a scís,
   Oscar ro bí a lám dess.

3. Tarlaic Oscar airchur n-oll
   co fergach, lonn immar léo,
   coro marb Cairpre úa Cuinn,
   rias-ra-gíallsatar gluinn gléo.

4. Amansi móra na mac
   fúaratar a mbas don gléo;
   gair siu condristais a n-airm
   roptar lía a mmairb inna mbéo.

5. Missi fodéin isin tress
   leith andess do Gabair glaiss;
   marbsa coecait laech fo dí;
   is missi ros bí dom baiss.

6. Arpetinn carbach fo chruch,
   in n-inaim ba ruth dom rog;
   ro marbainn torc i caill cháith,
   no sárginn én áith im og.

7. In t-ogam út fil isin chloich,
   imma torchratar na troich;
   dam maired Finn fichtib glonn,
   cían bad chuman in t-ogam.

## [ 88 ]
## Oisin's Dream

1. Tuilsitir mo derca súain;
   mo ruibni mam luibni ar ló;
   mo genum im dúais ro boí;
   ocus mo dúais imm ó.

2. Abdul físi armo-thá:
   dar chinnius co dían mo chuib
   ar chribais i lleirg ar art
   da ceird bracht co feic a cuill.

3. Tricha trethen dam co mnáib,
   ina taíb co tulmaing tuinn;
   tricha nena Finn na féic
   is séicse túas re fa thuinn.

4. Méit is ri habraid a derc;
   méit is ri mess a fert fó;
   selais mo genum a muin
   ocus mo chuib asa hó.

5. Cribais mara Talláin tair
   benais ri ail tairges tnú;
   mo leo úam faesum dum níad,
   mar túsa, ní tríath mar tú.

Glosses in ms.: 1.1 da chotlatar; mo súli. 1.2 mo
scíath; fam sleig. 1.3 mo chlaidiub im láim. 1.4
mo dorn im chlúais. 2.1 mor in t-aslingi atchon-
narc. 2.2 dar lecius; mo choin. 2.3 ar muicc; feoil.
2.4 saill furri corrici a fíacail; a carpait. 3.1 traiged;
co mbróic. 3.2 co moing a sróna. 3.3 ordlach; na
fíaccail. 3.4 na sailli; iss ed ro buí asa cinn immach
dá fíacail. 4.1 comméit ri coiri mór cach súil dí. 4.2
comméit ri tolaig a lecht ocus si féin na ligi. 4.3
tescaid mo chlaideb a munel. 4.4 mo chú asa clúais.
5.1 mucc. 5.2 ri cloich ris mbenann tonn. 5.3 armo
chommus féin. 5.4 ní lac immar tú.

## [ 91 ]
## Loch Silenn

Loch Sílend,
  is mairg nod n-ib ara bíad!
Ro llín Cairpre di chennaib
conid crú co rice a grían.

## [ 92 ]
## Ainmire mac Setna

Femen in tan ro boí rí
  nirbo mennot nach detlai;
indiu is forderg a lí
  la hAinmire mac Setnai.

## [ 96 ]
## On the Death
## of Mael Fothartaig

Ní diliu
nach rí limsa alaliu,
  ó bretha Mael Fothartaig
ina geimen do Dairiu.

## [ 97 ]
## On the Death of Aed mac Colgan,
## King of Leinster

Int Áed issin úir
  in rí issind róim,
int énán dil déin
  le Cérán i Clóin.

## [ 98 ]
## Cuchuimne

1. Cuchuimne
  ro leg suithe co druimne;
alleith n-aill h-íaratha
  ro leici an chaillecha.

2. Ando Coincuimne ro mboí
  imrúalaid de conid soí;
ro leic caillecha hi faill,
  ro leig alaill i rith mboí.

## [ 99 ]
## The Drowning of Niall Son of Aed

1. Mallacht ort, a Challainn chrúaid,
  a ṡrúaim amail ceó do ṡléib,
do riomart écc dá cach leith,
  for dreich nithaig níam guirm Neill.

2. Ni caraim in uisci n-dúabais,
  imteit sech toeb m'arais,
a Callainn ce nomaíde
  mac mná baíde ro bádais.

## [ 100 ]
## Kenneth Son of Conaing
## Is Executed by Drowning

1. Monúar a doine maithi,
  ba ferr a laithi cluichi;
mór líach Cinaeth mac Conaing
  hi lomand dochum cuithi.

2. Íar na cuimrech isin rían,
  mór líach ro cecht ar an tslúaig,
oc aiccsin a airrbi báin
  forsan tráig os Aingi úair.

## [ 101 ]
## Death of Princes

1. Rúaidri Manann minn n-áine
  Aed a crichaib Cinntíre,
Donnchad domna finn flatha,
  Garbsith minn Macha míne.

2. Ó do rálai, ar m'aire,
  fogerr crícha mo chride;
lecca húara íar n-aire
  baile for barrfinn bile.

# Notes

## ABBREVIATIONS

a: column 1.

*Acal.*: *Acallam na Senórach*, ed. and trans. Standish O'Grady, in *Sil. Gad.* (1892); ed. Whitley Stokes, *Ir.T.* 4 (1900); *Stories from the Acallam*, ed. Myles Dillon, MMIS no. 23 (1970). SEE ALSO *Agal.*

*ACL*: *Archiv für Celtische Lexicographie*, ed. Whitley Stokes and Kuno Meyer (Halle, 1898–1907).

Advo. Lib.: Advocates' Library, Edinburgh.

*Agal.*: *Agallamh na Seanórach*, ed. Nessa Ní Shéaghdha, 3 vols. (Dublin, 1942 [vols. 1–2], 1945 [vol. 3]). SEE ALSO *Acal.*

*AI*: *Annals of Inisfallen*, ed. Sean mac Airt (Dublin, 1951).

*AIP*: *Selections from Ancient Irish Poetry*, trans. Kuno Meyer (London, 1911; new ed., London: Constable, 1959).

*AIr:frag.*: *Annals of Ireland: Three Fragments*, ed. John O'Donovan (Dublin: Irish Archaeological Celtic Society, 1860).

*Anec.*: *Anecdota from Irish MSS* (Halle, 1907–1911).

*AU*: *Annals of Ulster*, ed. W. M. Hennessy and Bartholomew MacCarthy (Dublin, 1893, 1895, 1901).

b: column 2.

*BB*: *Book of Ballymote*.

*BDLis*: *Book of the Dean of Lismore*.

*BL*: *Book of Lecan*.

*BLis*: *The Book of MacCarthaigh Riabhach, otherwise The Book of Lismore*, ed. R. A. S. Macalister (Dublin: Stationery Office, 1950).

BM: British Museum or British Library.

*BUM*: *Book of the Uí Máine*.

*CM*: *Celtic Miscellany*, trans. Kenneth Jackson (London: Routledge and Kegan Paul, 1951; rev. ed., Penguin, 1971, 1973).

*CS*: *Chronicum Scotorum*, ed. W. M. Hennessy (London, 1866).

dip: diplomatic edition.

*Dub. U. Mag.*: magazine of the University of Dublin.

*ECNP*: *Early Celtic Nature Poetry*, by Kenneth Jackson (Cambridge: Cambridge University Press, 1935).

*ECV*: *Early Celtic Versecraft*, by James Travis (Ithaca, N.Y.: Cornell University Press, 1973).

Edin.: Edinburgh.

*Éigse: A Journal of Irish Studies* (Dublin).

*EIL*: *Early Irish Lyrics*, by Gerard Murphy (Oxford: Clarendon Press, 1956; reprint, 1962).

*EIM*: *Early Irish Metrics*, by Gerard Murphy (Dublin: Royal Irish Academy, 1961).
*Ériu*: *The Journal of the School of Irish Learning* (Dublin).
*Et.C. Etudes Celtiques* (Paris).
EW: E. Windisch.
fac: facsimile.
*FM*: *Annals of Ireland by the Four Masters*, ed. John O'Donovan (Dublin, 1856).
fol: folio.
*4 Songs*: *Four Old-Irish Songs of Summer and Winter*, ed. and trans. Kuno Meyer (London, 1903).
Franc ms: a manuscript of the Former College of Irish Franciscans at Louvain, now at Killiney.
G and O'C: David Greene and Frank O'Connor.
GM: Gerard Murphy.
*GTIP*: *The Golden Treasury of Irish Poetry, A.D. 600–1200*, ed. and trans. David Greene and Frank O'Connor (London: Macmillan, 1967).
Harl.: Harleian ms in the British Library.
*IOI*: *An Introduction to Old Irish*, by R. P. M. Lehmann and W. P. Lehmann (New York: Modern Language Association, 1975).
Ir. Arch. Soc.: Irish Archaeological and Celtic Society, Dublin [Publications].
*Ir.T.*: *Irische Texte*, vol. 1, ed. E. Windisch; vols. 2–4, ed. E. Windisch and Whitley Stokes (Leipzig, 1880–1909).
*ISP*: *Irish Syllabic Poetry*, by Eleanor Knott (Dublin, 1957).
ITS: Irish Texts Society (London).
JC: James Carney.
KJ: Kenneth Jackson.
KM: Kuno Meyer.
Laud: Laud mss, Bodleian Library, Oxford,
*LB*: *Leabar Breac*. MS, RIA.
*LH*: *Liber Hymnorum*, ed. J. H. Bernard and Robert Atkinson (London, 1898). MS, TCD.
*LL*: *Book of Leinster*; MS, TCD; fac is a transcript; dip by R. I. Best and others.
*LU*: *Lebar na hUidre*, MS, RIA; dip by Osborn Bergin and R. I. Best (Dublin, 1929).
*Mart. of Tall.*: *Martyrology of Tallaght*, ed. R. I. Best and H. J. Lawlor (London, 1931). MS, TCD (part of *LL*).
*MCAI*: *On the Manners and Customs of the Ancient Irish*, by Eugene O'Curry (London, 1873).
*Metr. Dinn.*: *The Metrical Dinnsenchas*, ed. Edward Gwynn, Todd Lecture Series VIII (Dublin, 1906).
*MIL*: *Medieval Irish Lyrics*, by James Carney (Berkeley and Los Angeles: University of California Press, 1967).
MMIS: Medieval and Modern Irish Series, published by the Dublin Institute for Advanced Studies.
*MS.Mat.*: *Lectures on the Manuscript Materials of Ancient Irish History*, by Eugene O'Curry (Dublin, 1861).
NLI: National Library of Ireland, Dublin.
*OST*: *Ossianic Society Transactions* (Dublin).
*Ot.M.*: *Otia Merseiana* (Liverpool).
*PIM*: *A Primer of Irish Metrics*, by Kuno Meyer (Dublin, 1909).
r: recto.
Rawl: Rawlinson ms., Bodleian Library, Oxford.
*RC*: *Revue Celtique* (Paris).

*Reader*, Pokorny: *A Historical Reader of Old Irish*, ed. Julius Pokorny (Halle: Max Niemeyer, 1923).
*Reader*, Th.: *Old Irish Reader*, ed. Rudolf Thurneysen (Dublin: DIAS, 1949).
RIA: Royal Irish Academy.
*RIA Contrib.*: *Contributions to a Dictionary of the Irish Language* (Dublin).
*Sil. Gad.*: *Silva Gadelica*, ed. and trans. Standish O'Grady (London, 1892).
TCD: Trinity College, Dublin.
Th: Rudolf Thurneysen.
*Thes.P.*: *Thesaurus Palaeohibernicus*, ed. Whitley Stokes and John Strachan (Cambridge; 1901, 1903).
*Tig. Annals of Tigernach*, ed. Whitley Stokes, in *RC* 16–18 (1895–1897).
v: verso.
WS: Whitley Stokes.
*YBL*: *Yellow Book of Lecan*, MS, TCD; fac ed. Robert Atkinson (Dublin, 1896).
*ZCP*: *Zeitschrift für Celtische Philologie* (Halle).

1. The Bee (*Daith bech buide a úaim i n-úaim*). Ms: TCD H.3.18 612 a. Editions: *Bruchstücke*, no. 159, pp. 68–69; *GTIP*, no. 54.5, p. 206.
2. Blackbird of the Wilderness (*Ach, a luin, is buide duit*). Ms: entered in the top margin of *LB* across p. 36. Editions: *Bruchstücke*, no. 151, p. 66; *GTIP*, no. 54.3, p. 206; *MIL*, no. 24, p. 82.
3. The Little Blackbird (*Int én bec*). Mss: *BB* 295.5; *BUM*, fol 136v b 45. Editions: Th, *Ir.T.* 3, no. 167, p. 99; *Zu irischen Handschriften und Literaturdenkmälern*, p. 69; *Bruchstücke*, no. 150, p. 66; *EIL*, no. 5, p. 6; *GTIP*, no. 54.2, p. 206; JC, *Ériu* 22 (1971): 58.
4. The Blackbird Calls from the Willow (*Int én gaires asin tsail*). Mss: Occurs twice in the account of meters, *BB* 298 b 20, 303 a 44; TCD H.2.12, sec. 8, p. 14; Laud 610 90v b 14; RIA ms., *BUM* 138r b 25. Editions: Th, *Ir.T.* 3, no. 53, p. 19; no. 75, p. 47; *EIL*, no. 6, p. 6; *GTIP*, no. 54.4, p. 206.
5. Calendar of the Birds (*Énlaith betha bríg cen táir*). Mss: *LL* fac 356, top margin; Br 5100-4. Edition: *Mart. of Tall.*, p. 94. St 4 is defective in both mss. For an explanation of the text (see Appendix) and translations, see *Et.C.* 17 (1980): 197–200.
6. Ocean (*Fégaid úaib*). Mss: *BB* 302 b 2; Laud 610. Editions: *Bruchstücke*, no. 149, p. 65; *Ir.T.* 3, no. 24, p. 38 (Laud); no. 187, p. 102 (*BB*); *GTIP*, no. 54.1, p. 205; *MIL*, no. 16, p. 40; *IOI*, p. 138; JC, *Ériu* 22 (1971): 56.
7. Storm on the Great Moor (*Úar ind adaig i Móin Móir*). Ms: *BB* 289 a 6. Editions: *Ir.T.* 3, no. 2, p. 67; *Bruchstücke*, p. 67; *GTIP*, no. 54.4, p. 206; *IOI*, p. 148.
8. A Great Storm at Sea (*Anbthine mór ar muig Lir*). Ms: Laud 610, fol 10 a 2. Editions: KM, *Ot.M.* 2 (1900–1901): 80–83; *GTIP*, no. 29, pp. 126–129. Notes: Michael O'Brien, *Et.C.* 3 (1939): 367–368; trans. KJ, *ECNP*, no. 32, pp. 30–31; *CM*, no. 17, pp. 70–71.
9. Winter Has Come (*Táinic gaimred co ngainni*). Mss: TCD H.3.18 624.661; H.4.22 67 c. Edition: *Bruchstücke*, no. 156, pp. 67–68.
10. Winter (*Scél lem dúib*). Mss: *LU* 11 b 20 (dip 850–865); Rawl. B 502, fol 58r a 13 (fac, p. 103); TCD H.2.16 col. 694.8. Editions: WS, *RC* 20 (1899): 258; *LH* 1: 174; *4 Songs*, p. 15; Pokorny, *Reader*, p. 16; *EIL*,

no. 53, pp. 160–161; *GTIP*, no. 21, p. 98; *MIL*, no. 6, pp. 10–13; trans only, *AIP*, p. 56; *ECNP*, no. 27, p. 26.

11. Winter Cold (*Fuit, fuit!*) Mss: Harl. 5280, fol 35 a; RIA 23 N 10, p. 13. Editions (Harl. only): KM, *RC* 11 (1890): 130–134; *GTIP*, no. 31, pp. 134–136.

12. Forever Cold (*Fúit co bráth!*). Mss: *LL* 208 a (dip 4: 1006, lines 29435–29450); Rawl. B 502, fol 59 b 2–60 a 1. Editions: Heinrich Zimmer, *Göttingische gelehrte Anzeigen* (1887), no. 5, pp. 184–185; *4 Songs*, p. 18; JC, *MIL*, no. 11, pp. 22–24; trans. KJ, *ECNP*, no. 29, p. 26. St 1 (especially in *LL*) is like st 2 of "Winter Cold."

13. The Worst and Best Weather (*Hed is annsam do rímaib*). Ms: Rawl. B 502. Editions: WS, *RC* 20 (1899): 256 (*Amra Choluim Chille*).

14. Slieve Cua (*Slíab cúa cúanach corrach dub*). Ms: BB 292 a 20. Editions: *Bruchstücke*, no. 153, p. 66; Th, *Ir.T.* 3, no. 99, p. 87. Trans. only, *ECNP*, no. 20, p. 19.

15. Summer Has Come (*Táinic sam slán sóer*). Mss: Rawl. B 502, fol 59 b 2–60 a 1 (fac 106). In attempting to determine the meaning of *snomh* in *Buile Shuibhne*, James George O'Keeffe cites the first two lines of the last stanza from RIA ms C.iii.2, fol 10 a. Editions: *4 Songs*, pp. 20–23; *GTIP*, no. 32, pp. 137–139; JC, *Ériu* 22 (1971): 43–45, trans. 46–47. JC treats this as accentual, not syllabic verse.

16–19. The Four Seasons (from *The Guesting of Aithirne*): 16. Autumn (*Ráithe fó foiss fogamar*). 17. Winter (*Dubaib ráithib rogeimred*). 18. Spring (*Glass úar errach aigide*). 19. Summer (*Fó sín samrad síthaister*). Mss: *LL* 118 a (dip 2: 436–437, lines 13621–13635); Harl. 5280, fol 77 a; RIA 23 N 10. Editions: KM, *Ériu* 7 (1910): 1–9; Th, *Ériu* 7 (1910): 196–199; *GTIP*, no. 33, pp. 140–142; KJ gives a translation and helpful notes, *ECNP*, no. 31, pp. 28–29, notes pp. 45–46.

20. King of Stars (*A Rí rinn*). Mss: Br 5100-4; Franc ms A 9, p. 39. Editions: KM, *ZCP* 1 (1897): 327; *GTIP*, no. 26.11, p. 113; *IOI*, p. 133.

21. The Wright (*A mo Choimdiu cid do-génsa*). Ms: Laud 610, fol 10 a 32. Editions: KM, *Ot.M.* 2 (1900–1901): 78; *GTIP*, no. 53.3, p. 202.

22. Adoration of the Creator (*Adram in Coimdid*). Mss: BB 303 a 5; Laud 610, fol 90r b 27–28. Editions: Th, *Ir.T.* 3, no. 54, p. 43; *EIL*, no. 4, p. 160.

23. Tears of Repentance (*A Dé, tuc dam topur ndér*). Ms: Franc ms A 9, p. 40. Editions: JC, *Éigse* 1 (1939): 248; P. Grosjean, *ZCP* 18 (1930): 300; *MIL*, no. 30, p. 78; *IOI*, p. 146.

24. Writing in the Wood (*Dom-farcai fidbaide fál*). Ms: St. Gall ms 904, lower margins, pp. 203–204 (Priscian's treatise on Latin grammar). Editions: *Thes.P.* 2: 290; *EIL*, no. 2, p. 4; *GTIP*, no. 18, p. 84; *MIL*, no. 9, p. 22; Th, *Reader* (Irish text only), p. 39.

25. Speaking God's Praise (*Mo labrad*). Mss: BM, Add. 30512, fol 32 b; TCD H.1.11, fol 140 a. Editions: KM, *ZCP* 12 (1918): 297; *EIL*, no. 28, p. 64.

26. Alone by Choice (*Glé limsa, a Choimdiu cen chol*). Ms: Rawl. B 502. Edition: WS, *RC* 20 (1899): 252.

27. God's House (*M'airiuclán hi Túaim Inbir*). Ms: Monastery of St. Paul in Carinthia preserves the unique ms. Editions: *Thes.P.* 2: 294; EW, *Ir.T.* 1: 318–319; Th, *Reader* (English), pp. 39–40; *EIL*, no. 43, p. 112; trans. *ECNP*, no. 1, p. 3, notes pp. 122–123.

28. The Weary Scribe (*Is scíth mo chrob ón scríbainn*). Ms: Laud 615, p. 55. Editions: KM, *Gaelic Journal* 8 (1889): 49; *ZCP* 12 (1918): 8; *EIL*, no. 33, p. 70; *GTIP*, no. 39, p. 159.

29. Colum Cille Leaving Ireland (*Fil súil nglais*). Mss: *LU* 5 a (dip 11: 307–310); Rawl. B 502, fol 54r a 17ff. Editions: *ZCP* 9 (1913): 284 (Andrew Kelleher, *Betha Coluimb Chille*); *EIL*, no. 29, p. 64; *MIL*, no. 36, p. 86.
30. The Little Bell (*Clocán binn*). Mss: TCD H.2.12, sec. 8, 13 b 13. Editions: Th, *Ir.T.* 3: 16; *EIL*, no. 3, p. 4; *GTIP*, no. 26.10, p. 113.
31. Prayers to Save and Shelter (*Cid lúath cach gadur glan glé*). Ms: Franc ms A, fol 44 b. Editions: P. Grosjean, *ZCP* 18 (1930): 300; JC, *Éigse* 1 (1940): 243–244.
32. Hymn to Saint Brigit (*Brigit bé bithmaith*). Mss: TCD E 42; Franc ms F 4. Editions: *Liber Hymnorum*, in *Thes.P.* 2: 325–326; EW, *Ir.T.* 1 (1880): 25–26; James Travis, *ECV*, pp. 64–66.
33. The Transitory World (*Ná luig, ná luig*). Ms: NLI Gaelic ms 1. Edition: JC, *MIL*, no. 17, pp. 40–42 (a note mentions single stanzas in two other mss).
34. To Find God (*Techt do Róim*). Ms: *Codex Boernerianus*, Munich. Editions: *Thes.P.* 2: 296; Th, *Reader*, p. 41; *GTIP*, no. 26.8, p. 112; *MIL*, no. 32, p. 80.
35. Who Knows of His Death? (*In ba maiten, in ba fuin*). Mss: *YBL*, col 293–294 (across bottom margin) (fac 305); Laud 610, p. 411 a; and *LB*, p. 172; fac across bottom margin in all three. Editions: KM, *Gaelic Journal* 4 (1885): 114–115; *ZCP* 9 (1913): 479 n. 2; *PIM*, p. 9, sec. 19 (1) (a); *EIM*, pp. 28–29 n. 3.
36. Mo Ling Offends None (*Tan bím eter mo sruithe*). Mss: Laud 610 a; Franc ms A 7, p. 47 b 15ff; *LB*, p. 90.57f. Editions: WS, *Félire Óengusso* (London, 1880), p. ciii a (Mo Ling's feast day June 17); *EIL*, no. 13, p. 32.
37. Mael Isu O'Brolchan's Primer (*A Chrínóc, cubaid do cheól*). Ms: Franc ms A 9. Editions: KM, *ZCP* 6 (1908): 266; JC, *Éigse* 4 (1943–1944): 280–283; *GTIP*, no. 42, pp. 167–169; *MIL*, no. 29, pp. 74–78.
38. Prayer for Protection (*Día lim fri cach sním*). Mss: RIA 23 N 10, p. 19; B iv 2, p. 137; 23 E 16, p. 337; Laud 615, p. 91. Editions: KM, *ACL* 3 (1907): 6–7; Andrew O'Kelleher, *Ériu* 4 (1910): 235–239; *EIL*, no. 10, pp. 22–26.
39. The Hermit's Wish (*Dúthracar a Maic Dé bí*). Ms: RIA 23 N 10, p. 95. Editions: KM, *Ériu* 1 (1904): 39; *EIL*, no. 12, p. 28; *GTIP*, no. 35, p. 148; trans. KJ, *ECNP*, no. 3, pp. 4–5.
40. The Hermit (*M'Óenurán im aireclán*). Mss: RIA 23 N 10, p. 20; NLI, no. 7, col 26; RIA B iv 2, p. 138; Franc ms A 9, p. 40. Editions (23 N 10): John Strachan, *Ériu* 1 (1904): 138; KM, *Ériu* 2 (1905): 55–56; *EIL*, no. 9, p. 18.
41. Colum Cille in Exile (*Mellach lem bith i n-ucht ailiun*). Mss: Br 5100-4; Edin. ms 5, fol 10 a. Editions: (BR) KM, *ZCP* 5 (1905): 496–497; (Edin.) Donald MacKinnon, *Catalogue of Gaelic MSS* (Edin.: W. Brown, 1912), pp. 81–82. Attributed to Colum Cille, T. F. O'Rahilly, *Measgra Danta* (Dublin and Cork: Cork University Press, 1927) 2, no. 42, pp. 120–121. Trans., William Forbes Skene, *Celtic Scotland* (Edin.: D. Douglas, 1887) 2: 92–93 (gives O'Curry's trans. from *MCAI*); KJ, *ECNP*, no. 6, pp. 9–10.
42. Meditation Gone Astray (*Is mebul dom imrádud*). Mss: *LB*, p. 262; RIA B iv 2, p. 141. Editions: KM, *Ériu* 3 (1907): 15; *EIL*, no. 17, p. 38; *GTIP*, no. 34, p. 144. In st 4, line 3, *tre dochraite dimbithe* (*LB*), I have followed Greene and O'Connor in reversing the order of words to keep the rime. I translate with a suggestion from *RIA Contrib.*, "uncleared places."
43. Colum Cille and Guaire (*Déna, a Gúaire, maith um ní*). Ms: Laud 615, p. 33. Edition: KM, *King and Hermit* (London: Nutt, 1901), Appendix 1.

44. Guaire and Marban (*A Marbáin, a díthrubaig*). Ms: Harl. 5280, fol 42 b.
    Editions: KM, *King and Hermit* (London: Nutt, 1901); *ZCP* 3 (1901);
    trans., *AIP*, pp. 47–50; GM, *EIL*, no. 8, pp. 10–18; JC, *MIL*, no. 27, pp.
    66–72; trans. and notes, KJ, *ECNP*, no. 5, pp. 5–8. None of these is a
    complete translation; for an explanation of the present rendering see *ZCP* 36
    (1977): 96–111. The "house of skins" (*tech lethoir*) is a literal translation.
    GM mentions a "book satchel" (*EIL*, p. 77), but elsewhere this is *tech libair*
    "house of books." In the Irish climate a house of mud and wattles would be
    greatly improved by a leather covering, and Marban is not famous for his
    book-learning.

45. Daniel O'Liathaite Rebukes a Temptress (*A ben, bennacht fort—ná ráid*). Mss:
    *LL* 278 a 21ff (dip 5: 1221, pp. 36215–36238); TCD H.3.18, p. 731.
    Editions: EW, *Berichte der Königliche Sächsische Gesellschaft der Wissenschaften*
    (Leipzig, 1890), p. 86; KM, *Ériu* 1 (1904): 67–68; *EIL*, no. 7, p. 6; JC,
    *Éigse* 13 (1970): 297–300 (important notes on Murphy's text).

46. The Old Woman of Beare (*Aithbe damsa bés mora*). Mss: TCD H.3.18, p. 42
    b; ibid., p. 764; H.4.22, p. 44; H.5.6, p. 187; NLI Gaelic ms 7 (formerly
    Phillips 9748), col 23. Editions: KM, *Ot.M.* 1: 119ff; GM, *Proceedings of the
    RIA* 55.83–106; Osborn Bergin, *Ériu* 2 (1905): 240–241; *EIL*, no. 34,
    pp. 74–82; *GTIP*, no. 9, pp. 48–55; *MIL*, no. 15, pp. 28–40.

47. Liadan Loses Cuirithir (*Cen áinius*). Mss: TCD H.3.18, pp. 759ff; BM,
    Harl. 5280 26 a ff. Editions: KM, *Liadain and Curithir* (London: D. Nutt,
    1902); Pokorny, *Reader*, pp. 16–17; *EIL*, no. 35, pp. 82–85; *GTIP*, no.
    13, pp. 72–74; *MIL*, no. 13, pp. 24–28.

48. Eve (*Mé Éba, ben Adaim uill*). Mss: RIA B iv 2, fol 146; BM, Add. 19995,
    fol 2 b (lower right). Editions: KM, *Ériu* 3 (1907): 148; *EIL*, no. 21,
    p. 50; *GTIP*, no. 38, p. 157; *MIL*, no. 28, p. 72.

49. Little Jesus (*Ísucán*). Mss: *LB*, fol 79; Laud 610, fol 61 r a; *BL*, fac 166v ca.
    34–38; Franc ms A 7, fol 7r a; RIA 23 P 3, fol 2v; Br 5100-4 (ca. p. 80
    microfilm). Editions: WS, *Félire Oengusso* (London, 1880), p. xxxv; 2d ed.
    (1905), p. 44; *EIL*, no. 11, p. 26; *GTIP*, no. 23, p. 102; *MIL*, no. 26,
    p. 64. This poem was obviously well known and is added in the margin of
    accounts of St. Ite, even when not in the original text. See mss.

50. Lament for Dinertach (*It é saigte gona súain*). Mss: Harl. 5280, fol 25 b. Edi-
    tions: KM, *Ériu* 2 (1905): 15ff; *EIL*, no. 36, pp. 86–89; *GTIP*, no. 16,
    pp. 78–80. See JC, *Éigse* 13 (1970): 227–242, and R. P. M. Lehmann,
    *Et.C.* 15 (1978): 549–551.

51. The Sweetheart (*Cride é*). Ms: *BB*. Editions: Th, *Ir.T.* 3, no. 177, p. 100;
    *Bruchstücke*, no. 160, p. 69; *EIM*, p. 59; *GTIP*, no. 26.4, p. 112; *MIL*, no.
    14, p. 28.

52. A Girl Sings (*Gel cech núa—sásad nglé!*). Ms: *LL*, fol 121 a margin. Edition:
    *GTIP*, no. 53.5, p. 203.

53. Loveloneliness (*Och is fada atáim a-muigh*). KM, *ZCP* 13 (1921): 18, cites
    Franc ms A 9.1, but not discoverable there nor in Fr. Paul Grosjean's de-
    scription of Ms A 9, *Ériu* 10 (1926–1928): 160–169, nor in the catalogue
    of the Franciscan Library, 1969. KM gives no translation.

54. Cat and Scholar (*Messe ocus Pangur bán*). Ms: From a ms from the Monastery
    of St. Paul in Carinthia. Editions: *Thes.P.* 2: 293–294; *EIL*, no. 1, p. 2;
    *GTIP*, no. 17, p. 81; Th, *Reader* (English), pp. 40–41.

55. "What, All My Pretty Chickens?" (*Cumthach labras in lonsa*). Ms: *LB* 186 a
    1. Editions: KM, *Gaelic Journal* 4 (1890): 42–43; Eleanor Knott, *ISP*,
    p. 29; *GTIP*, no. 37, p. 154. Note on the translation: Greene and O'Con-

nor open st 8 with "A fearful host came like a blast," but though the fairy
host is more often *sidslúag* than *slúagsid*, "fearful" seems to be merely an
interpretation. I assume that the speaker's family was wiped out by disease,
here blamed on the fairies, with his helplessness like that of the bird.

56. The Viking Threat (*Is aicher in gáeth in-nocht*). Ms: St. Gall, Priscian. Edi-
tions: *Thes.P.* 2: 290; Th, *Reader*, p. 39, *GTIP*, no. 26.9, p. 113; *MIL*,
no. 10, p. 22.

57. A Splendid Sword (*Luin oc elaib*). Mss: *LB*, *YBL*, etc.; *Cormac's Glossary*,
no. 69. Editions: WS, *ZCP* 19 (1933): 198; KM, *Anec.* 4: 7; James Travis,
*ECV*, p. 67 (from Frank O'Connor, *A Short History of Irish Literature* [New
York: Putnam, 1967]); JC, *Ériu* 22 (1971): 54.

58. The Necessity of Reading (*Cid glic fri hailchi úara*). Ms: Br 5100-4. Edition:
KM, *ZCP* 1 (1897): 327.

59. You See Your Own Faults in Others (*Cid becc—mét friget—do locht*). Ms: Br
5100-4. Edition: KM, *ZCP* 1 (1897): 327.

60. Broad-minded Etan (*Ní fetar*). Mss: *BB* 298 b 18–20; TCD H.2.12. Edi-
tions: Th, *Ir.T.* 3, no. 52, p. 19; *GTIP*, no. 26.2, p. 111; *IOI*, p. 133.

61. Satire on a Rustic (*Atá ben as-tír*). Mss: *LU* 8 a (dip 19.543–546); H.3.18,
611 a; Rawl. B 502, fol 56v a 3 (fac, p. 100). Editions: *Bruchstücke*, no. 77,
p. 34; *RC* 20 (1899): 158, sec. 7; *GTIP*, no. 26.1, p. 111.

62. Midir Summons Etain to Fairyland (*A bé find, in rega lim*). Mss: *LU* 131 b
(dip 330.10814–10871); NLI 4 (formerly Phillips ms 8244, col 994); st 5
only, TCD H.3.18, p. 606, end col 2. Editions: *EIL*, no. 41, pp. 104–106.

63. Fann's Farewell to Cu Chulainn (*Fégaid mac láechraidi Lir*). Mss: *LU* 50 a 1
(dip 124.3959–4010); TCD H.4.22.Editions: E. Windisch, *Ir.T.* 1: 197;
Myles Dillon, *Serglige Con Culainn*, MMIS, no. 24 (1953), pp. 26–28.

64. The Cry of the Sweetsounding Garb (*Gáir na Gairbe glaídbinne*). Ms: Br
5100-4, p. 52. Editions: Whitley Stokes, *Anec.* 2: 23–24; *CM*, no. 24,
pp. 78–79 (trans. of stt 1–10); *EIL*, no. 44, pp. 112–116.

65. The Snow Is Cold Tonight (*In-nocht is fúar in snechta*). Mss: RIA B iv 1; 23 K
44. Editions: J. G. O'Keeffe, ITS 12 (1913): 29–33; MMIS, 1 (1932):
15–17.

66. My Night in Cell Derfile (*M'agaid i cCill Derffile*). Ms: RIA B iv 1; 23 K 44.
Editions: J. G. O'Keeffe, ITS 12 (1913): 35–37; MMIS 1 (1932): 19.

67. The Woman Who Reaps the Watercress (*A ben benus a birar*). Mss: RIA B iv
1; 23 K 44. Editions: J. G. O'Keeffe, ITS 12 (1913): 84–91; MMIS 1
(1932): 45–48. Suggested rearrangement: R. P. M. Lehmann, *Et.C.* 7
(1956): 123–127.

68. Suibne on a Snowy Night (*Mór múich i túsa in-nocht*). Mss: RIA B iv 1; 23 K
44. Editions: J. G. O'Keeffe, ITS 12 (1913): 118–123; MMIS 1 (1932):
63–64; *EIL*, no. 47, pp. 138–140.

69. The Cursed Banquet (*In chuit sin chaithise in-nocht*). Mss: *YBL*, col 324, fac
320 b 34; RIA B iv 1; 23 K 44. Editions: John O'Donovan, *Battle of Magh
Rath* (Dublin: Ir. Arch. Soc., 1842), pp. 30–33; Carl Marstrander, *Vid-
enskabs-Selskabets Skrifter* 2, Hist.-Filos. Klasse, no. 6 (1910), p. 10; R. P.
M. Lehmann, *Fled Dúin na nGéd*, MMIS 21 (1964), lines 273–288; trans.,
*Lochlann* 4 (1969): 139–140.

70. Ronan with His Dead Son (*Is úar fri clói ngaíthe*). Mss: *LL*, fol 272 b–273 a
(dip 5: 1198–1199, lines 35572–35597); TCD H.3.18 752. Editions:
KM, *RC* 13 (1892): 388–391; David Greene, *Fingal Ronan*, MMIS 16
(1955): 8–9, lines 168–192.

71. After Vengeance Ronan and the Hounds Lament His Son (*Ro-gab Eochaid*

*oenléni*). Mss: *LL* 273 a (dip 5: 1199–1200, lines 35601–35648); TCD H.3.18 753. Editions: KM, *RC* 13 (1892): 390–395; Greene, *Fingal Ronan*, MMIS 16 (1955): 9–10, lines 197–244.

72. Grainne in Love with Diarmait (*Fil duine*). Mss: Rawl. B 502, fol 56r b 28, fac p. 99; *LU*, fol 7v (dip 512–517); TCD E.4.2, fol 26 a (*Liber Hymnorum*); *YBL* H.2.17, col 686.39 (fac, p. 75 a 40–42); Egerton 1782 (BM), fol 6v b 13; RIA C.3.2, fol 7r b 42. Editions: WS, *RC* 20 (1899): 156; *EIL*, no. 54, p. 160; *GTIP*, no. 26.6, p. 112.

73. Grainne's Forest Fare (*Is maith do chuit, a Gráinne*). Ms.: Rawl. B 502. Edition: WS, *RC* 20 (1899): 264.

74. Sleepsong of Grainne (*Cotail becán becán bec*). Ms: Franc ms A 9, fol 44 b. Editions: Eoin MacNeill, *Duanaire Finn*, vol. 1, ITS 7 (1908), no. 33, p. 84; *EIL*, no. 55, pp. 160–164; *GTIP*, no. 48, pp. 184–186.

75. Caeilte Speaks of Finn (*Dámad ór in duille donn*). Ms: *BLis*, fol 159 b (fac 203 a). Editions: WS, *Ir.T.* 4: 4; *Sil Gad.* 1: 96; Dillon, *Acal.*, p. 4.

76. Arran (*Arann na n-aiged n-imda*). Mss: *BLis*, fol 161 b (fac 203 b); RIA 24 P 5, p. 172; 23 L 34, p. 258. Editions: WS, *Ir.T.* 4: 10–11; *Sil. Gad.* 1: 102; *Agal.* 1: 29–31; T. F. O'Rahilly, *Measgra Danta* (Dublin and Cork: Cork University Press, 1927) 1, no. 40, pp. 59–60; Dillon, *Acal.*, pp. 5–6; trans., *AIP*, p. 59.

77. Well of the Strand of Two Women (*A thopair Trága Dá Ban*). Ms: *BLis*, fol 159 b 1 (fac, 201v a 17). Editions: WS, *Ir.T.* 4: 3–4; *Sil. Gad.*, p. 96; Dillon, *Acal.*, pp. 3–4.

78. The Sons of Lugaid (*Trí tuile*). Mss: *BLis*, fol 162 a (fac, 207 a 24); *LL* 206 a (dip 4: 992, lines 29049–29088). Editions: WS, *Ir.T.* 4: 13–14; *Sil. Gad.*, p. 104; Dillon, *Acal.*, pp. 9–10; *Metr. Dinn.* 4: 368; *Agal.* 1: 38–39.

79. Creide's Lament for Cael (*Géisid cúan*). Mss: *BLis*, fol 207 a; Rawl. B 487, fol 17v. Editions: WS, *Ir.T.* 4: 24; *Sil. Gad.*, p. 113; KM, *Cath Finntrága* (Oxford, 1885), lines 994–1034; *Agal.* 1: 70–71; *ISP*, pp. 27–28; *EIL*, no. 49, pp. 148–150; Dillon, *Acal.*, pp. 16–18.

80. Beagles Bay on the Hill of Kings (*Guth gadair i cCnoc na Ríg*). Ms: Franc ms A 9, fol 44. Editions: Eoin MacNeill, *Duanaire Finn*, ITS 7 (1908), no. 32, p. 83. Notes by GM, *Duanaire Finn*, vol. 3, ITS 43 (1953). The *sid* (st 1, line 2) is a fairy hill, later also the fairies.

81. A Bell Rings on the Red Ridge (*Faíd cluic do-chúala i nDruim Deirg*). Ms: Franc ms A 9, fol 72. Editions: GM, *Duanaire Finn*, vol. 2, ITS 28 (1933), no. 53, pp. 178ff.

82. The Death of Finn's Hound Conbecc (*Trúag lem aided Chonbicce*). Mss: *BLis*, fol 174; Laud 610; Rawl. 487; RIA 24 P 5. Editions: WS, *Ir.T.* 4: 62–63; *Sil. Gad.*, p. 143; *Agal.* 1: 268–269.

83. Caeilte Sang of Strength Departed (*Bec in-nocht lúth mo dá lúa*). Ms: *LL* 208 a (dip 4: 1005). Edition: KM, *Ériu* 1 (1904): 72–73. The ms glosses difficult words of the Bérla na Filed ("language of poets"). KM assigns it to the first half of the twelfth century.

84. Caeilte Returns to the Mound of the Fian (*Forud na Fíann fás in-nocht*). Mss: *BLis*, fol 222v a; Laud 610, fol 129r; Franc ms A 20, p. 44 b; Rawl. 487, fol 34r. Editions: WS, *Ir.T.* 4: 95; *Sil. Gad.*, p. 168; *Agal.* 2: 152; *EIL*, no. 50, p. 152.

85. Music of the World (*Binn guth duine i dTír in Óir*). Ms: *BDLis*. Editions: T. F. O'Rahilly, *Measgra Danta* (Dublin and Cork: Cork University Press,

1927) 1: 87n; Neil Ross, *Heroic Poetry*, Scottish Gaelic Texts Society 3 (1939), no. 13, p. 82.

86. A Dreary Night in Elphin (*Is fada anocht i n-Oil Finn*). Mss: *BDLis*, fol 50; Franc ms A 20 b, 73v 4. Editions: T. F. O'Rahilly, *Measgra Danta* (Dublin and Cork: Cork University Press, 1927) 2, no. 71, pp. 182–183; GM, *Duanaire Finn*, vol. 2, ITS 28 (1933), no. 55, pp. 194–195; Neil Ross, *Heroic Poetry*, Scottish Gaelic Texts Society 3 (1939), no. 4, pp. 8–10. St 5 from Ross.

87. A Grave Marked with Ogam (*Ogum i llía, lía úas lecht*). Ms: LL 154 a (dip 3: 663). Editions: Nicholas O'Kearney, *Battle of Gabhra*, OST 1 (1894): 49–51; EW, *Ir.T.* 1 (1880): 158; *MCAI* 1: ccxii. All give O'Curry's trans. for this version; see *Et.C.* 17 (1980): 200–203.

88. Oisin's Dream (*Tuilsitir mo derca súain*). Mss: *LL* 208 a (dip 4: 1004); *BDLis*. Editions: E. Windisch, *Ir.T.* 1 (1880): 162–163; *RC* 2 (1875): 470; William Forbes Skene, introduction to Thomas McLauchlan, *The Dean of Lismore's Book* (Edin., 1862), p. lxxxiv; *Dub. U. Mag.* (1882) Dr. Anster trans. Heavily glossed in ms like no. 83, and also in Bérla na Filed.

89. Oisin Remembers Wilder Days (*Ro loiscit na lámasa*). Ms: RIA D iv 2, fol 88r (66) col 2. Editions: KM, *RC* 6 (1884): 185–186; *RC* 17 (1896): 319; KM, *Fianaigecht* (Dublin, 1910), p. xxviii; *EIL*, no. 57, p. 166. The trans. of the last st follows a suggestion in GM's notes.

90. Oisin Laments His Youth (*Do bádussa úair*). Ms: Franc ms A 20, fol 43 a. Editions: Eoin MacNeill, *Duanaire Finn*, vol. 1, ITS 7 (1908), no. 25, p. 80); *EIL*, no. 58, p. 168.

91–101. Poems from the Chronicles. These are given in chronological order; references are listed after each poem. Here are given the editions of the chronicles referred to and then any further editions or other comments if the chronicle and year are not enough: *Annals of Ireland by the Four Masters* (*FM*), ed. John O'Donovan (Dublin, 1856), mss TCD and RIA; *Annals of Ireland: Three Fragments* (*AIr:frag.*), ed. John O'Donovan (Dublin: Irish Archaeological and Celtic Society, 1860); *Chronicum Scotorum* (*CS*), ed. W. M. Hennessy (Dublin, 1901), ms TCD H.1.18; *Annals of Tigernach* (*Tig.*), ed. WS, *RC* 17 (1896): 6–33, 116–263, 337–420, ms Rawl. B 488; *Annals of Ulster* (*AU*), ed. W. M. Hennessy and Bartholomew MacCarthy (Dublin, 1901), mss TCD H.1.8, Rawl. B 489; *Annals of Ireland* (*AI*), ed. Sean mac Airt (Dublin, 1951), ms Rawl. B 503.

93. His Queen Laments Aed Son of Ainmire (*Batar inmuine in trí toíb*). *Bruchstücke*, no. 89, p. 38; Myles Dillon, *Early Irish Literature* (Chicago, 1948), p. 155; Myles Dillon and Nora K. Chadwick, *Celtic Realms* (London: Weidenfeld and Nicolson, 1967), p. 230; rev. ed. (London: Cardinal Sphere Books, 1973), p. 285; JC, *MIL*, no. 12, p. 24.

94. On The Death of Aed mac Colgan, King of Airther (*Ro boí tan*). WS, *RC* 20 (1899): 276; *Bruchstücke*, no. 90, p. 38; *GTIP*, no. 25.1, p. 107.

95. The Drowning of Conaing (*Tonna mora mórglana*). Pokorny, *Reader*, pp. 4–5; *Bruchstücke*, no. 92, p. 39; *GTIP*, no. 25.3, p. 108.

96. On the Death of Mael Fothartaig (*Ní diliu*). *Bruchstücke*, no. 97, p. 43.

97. On the Death of Aed mac Colgan, King of Leinster (*Int Aed issin úir*). *AIr:frag.* contains only the first line.

98. Cuchuimne (*Cuchuimne*). In *FM* these verses are given as Adamnan's statement to Cuchuimne and his reply, with appropriate changes of tense.

99. The Drowning of Niall Son of Aed (*Mallacht ort, a Challainn chrúaid*). St 2 is only in *FM*.

# Index of First Lines (Irish)

[Strictly alphabetical, ignoring word divisions, apostrophes, and *h* before a vowel. Dagger indicates Irish text is included in Appendix.]

*A bé find, in rega lim* (Midir Summons Etain to Fairyland)  62
*A ben, bennacht fort—ná ráid* (Daniel O'Liathaite Rebukes a Temptress)  45
*A ben benus a birar* (The Woman Who Reaps the Watercress)  67†
*Ach, a luin, is buide duit* (Blackbird of the Wilderness)  2
*A Chrínóc, cubaid do cheól* (Mael Isu O'Brolchan's Primer)  37
*A Dé, tuc dam topur ndér* (Tears of Repentance)  23
*Adram in Coimdid* (Adoration of the Creator)  22
*Aithbe damsa bés mora* (The Old Woman of Beare)  46
*A Marbáin, a díthrubaig* (Guaire and Marban)  44†
*A mo Choimdiu, cid do-génsa* (The Wright)  21
*Anbthine mór ar muig Lir* (A Great Storm at Sea)  8
*Arann na n-aiged n-imda* (Arran)  76†
*A Rí rinn* (King of Stars)  20
*Atá ben as-tír* (Satire on a Rustic)  61
*A thopair Trága Dá Ban* (Well of the Strand of Two Women)  77†

*Batar inmuine in trí toíb* (His Queen Laments Aed Son of Ainmire)  93
*Bec in-nocht lúth mo dá lúa* (Caeilte Sang of Strength Departed)  83†
*Binn guth duine i dTír in Óir* (Music of the World)  85†
*Brigit bé bithmaith* (Hymn to Saint Brigit)  32†

*Cen áinius* (Liadan Loses Cuirithir)  47
*Cid becc—mét friget—do locht* (You See Your Own Faults in Others)  59†
*Cid glic fri hailchi úara* (The Necessity of Reading)  58†
*Cid lúath cach gadur glan glé* (Prayers to Save and Shelter)  31†
*Clocán binn* (The Little Bell)  30
*Cotail becán becán bec* (Sleepsong of Grainne)  74
*Cride é* (The Sweetheart)  51
*Cuchuimne* (Cuchuimne)  98†
*Cumthach labras in lonsa* ("What, All My Pretty Chickens?")  55

*Daith bech buide a úaim i n-úaim* (The Bee)  1
*Dámad ór in duille donn* (Caeilte Speaks of Finn)  75†
*Déna, a Gúaire, maith um ní* (Colum Cille and Guaire)  43†
*Día lim fri cach sním* (Prayer for Protection)  38

*Do bádussa úair* (Oisin Laments His Youth)   90
*Dom-farcai fidbaide fál* (Writing in the Wood)   24
*Dubaib ráithib rogeimred* (Winter [from *The Guesting of Aithirne*])   17
*Dúthracar, a Maic Dé bí* (The Hermit's Wish)   39

*Hed is annsam do rímaib* (The Worst and Best Weather)   13†
*Énlaith betha bríg cen táir* (Calendar of the Birds)   5†

*Faíd cluic do-chúala i nDruim Deirg* (A Bell Rings on the Red Ridge)   81†
*Fégaid mac láechraidi Lir* (Fann's Farewell to Cu Chulainn)   63†
*Fégaid úaib* (Ocean)   6
*Femen in tan ro boí rí* (Ainmire mac Setna)   92†
*Fil duine* (Grainne in Love with Diarmait)   72
*Fil súil nglais* (Colum Cille Leaving Ireland)   29
*Forud na Fíann fás in-nocht* (Caeilte Returns to the Mound of the Fian)   84
*Fó sín samrad síthaister* (Summer [from *The Guesting of Aithirne*])   19
*Fuit co bráth!* (Forever Cold)   12
*Fuit, fuit!* (Winter Cold)   11

*Gáir na Gairbe glaídbinne* (The Cry of the Sweetsounding Garb)   64
*Géisid cúan* (Creide's Lament for Cael)   79
*Gel cech núa—sásad nglé!* (A Girl Sings)   52
*Glass úar errach aigide* (Spring [from *The Guesting of Aithirne*])   18
*Glé limsa, a Choimdiu cen chol* (Alone by Choice)   26†
*Guth gadair i cCnoc na Ríg* (Beagles Bay on the Hill of Kings)   80†

*In ba maiten, in ba fuin* (Who Knows of His Death?)   35†
*In chuit sin chaithise in-nocht* (The Cursed Banquet)   69†
*In-nocht is fúar in snechta* (The Snow Is Cold Tonight)   65†
*Int Áed issin úir* (On the Death of Aed mac Colgan, King of Leinster)   97†
*Int én bec* (The Little Blackbird)   3
*Int én gaires asin tsail* (The Blackbird Calls from the Willow)   4
*Is aicher in gáeth in-nocht* (The Viking Threat)   56
*Is fada anocht i n-Oil Finn* (A Dreary Night in Elphin)   86†
*Is maith do chuit, a Gráinne* (Grainne's Forest Fare)   73†
*Is mebul dom imrádud* (Meditation Gone Astray)   42
*Is scíth mo chrob ón scríbainn* (The Weary Scribe)   28
*Is úar fri clói ngaíthe* (Ronan with His Dead Son)   70
*Ísucán* (Little Jesus)   49
*It é saigte gona súain* (Lament for Dinertach)   50

*Loch Sílend* (Loch Silenn)   91†
*Luin oc elaib* (A Splendid Sword)   57†

*M'agaid i cCill Derffile* (My Night in Cell Derfile)   66†
*M'airiuclán hi Túaim Inbir* (God's House)   27
*Mallacht ort, a Challainn chrúaid* (The Drowning of Niall Son of Aed)   99†
*Mé Éba, ben Adaim uill* (Eve)   48
*Mellach lem bith i n-ucht ailiun* (Colum Cille in Exile)   41†
*Messe ocus Pangur bán* (Cat and Scholar)   54
*M'óenurán im aireclán* (The Hermit)   40
*Mo labrad* (Speaking God's Praise)   25

*Monúar a doine maithi* (Kenneth Son of Conaing Is Executed by Drowning)   100†
*Mor múich ı túsa ın-nocht* (Suibne on a Snowy Night)   68

*Ná luig, ná luig* (The Transitory World)   33
*Ní diliu* (On the Death of Mael Fothartaig)   96†
*Ní fetar* (Broad-minded Etan)   60

*Och is fada atáim a-muigh* (Loveloneliness)   53†
*Ogum i llía, lía úas lecht* (A Grave Marked with Ogam)   87†

*Ráithe fó foiss fogamar* (Autumn [from *The Guesting of Aithirne*])   16
*Ro boí tan* (On the Death of Aed mac Colgan, King of Airther)   94
*Ro-gab Eochaid oenléni* (After Vengeance Ronan and the Hounds Lament His Son)   71
*Ro loiscit na lámasa* (Oisin Remembers Wilder Days)   8ϛ
*Rúaidri Manann minn n-áine* (Death of Princes)   101†

*Scél lem dúib* (Winter)   10
*Slíab cúa cúanach corrach dub* (Slieve Cua)   14†

*Táinic gaimred co ngainni* (Winter Has Come)   9†
*Táinic sam slán sóer* (Summer Has Come)   15
*Tan bím eter mo ṡruithe* (Mo Ling Offends None)   36†
*Techt do Róim* (To Find God)   34
*Tonna mora mórglana* (The Drowning of Conaing)   95
*Trí tuile* (The Sons of Lugaid)   78†
*Trúag lem aided Chonbicce* (The Death of Finn's Hound Conbecc)   82†
*Tuilsitir mo derca súain* (Oisin's Dream)   88†

*Úar ind adaig i Móin Móir* (Storm on the Great Moor)   7